THE RIGHT CAT
FOR ME

**Andrew De Prisco
and James B. Johnson**
Featuring Photographer Isabelle Francais

KW-238

Title page: *As this handsome youngster can attest, the Abyssinian is the right choice of any worthy cat owner. Owner, Gail Christie.*

© 1996 by T.F.H. Publications, Inc.

Distributed in the UNITED STATES to the Pet Trade by T.F.H. Publications, Inc., One T.F.H. Plaza, Neptune City, NJ 07753; distributed in the UNITED STATES to the Bookstore and Library Trade by National Book Network, Inc. 4720 Boston Way, Lanham MD 20706; in CANADA to the Pet Trade by H & L Pet Supplies Inc., 27 Kingston Crescent, Kitchener, Ontario N2B 2T6; Rolf C. Hagen Inc., 3225 Sartelon St. Laurent-Montreal Quebec H4R 1E8; in CANADA to the Book Trade by Vanwell Publishing Ltd., 1 Northrup Crescent, St. Catharines, Ontario L2M 6P5 ; in ENGLAND by T.F.H. Publications, PO Box 15, Waterlooville PO7 6BQ; in AUSTRALIA AND THE SOUTH PACIFIC by T.F.H. (Australia), Pty. Ltd., Box 149, Brookvale 2100 N.S.W., Australia; in NEW ZEALAND by Brooklands Aquarium Ltd. 5 McGiven Drive, New Plymouth, RD1 New Zealand; in Japan by T.F.H. Publications, Japan—Jiro Tsuda, 10-12-3 Ohjidai, Sakura, Chiba 285, Japan; in SOUTH AFRICA by Lopis (Pty) Ltd., P.O. Box 39127, Booysens, 2016, Johannesburg, South Africa. Published by T.F.H. Publications, Inc.
MANUFACTURED IN THE UNITED STATES OF AMERICA
BY T.F.H. PUBLICATIONS, INC.

For Frederick

and

his beloved

Catherine

All for the view. This domestic feline is contentedly up a tree.

Foreword

THE RIGHT CAT FOR ME is what everyone should read before getting a cat. Andrew De Prisco and his co-author Jim Johnson in this book give the necessary facts for the consumer to think about. Andrew has a full understanding of the nature of the feline and it is evident throughout the text and captions. His writing is from experience and personal knowledge.

Happiness and successful ownership of a cat greatly depend on "the right cat". The amount of coat to care for, the voice and behavior of the cat must suit your personality. All these things lend themselves to a happy relationship for both cat and owner.

Even though breeders and catteries claim their breed is the best, perhaps it is only best for them. The right breed for you will surely be enhanced by reading *THE RIGHT CAT FOR ME* first.

Richard H. Gebhardt
International All-Breed Judge

The Maine Coon gets up on his twos to help you choose the right cat for you! Owner, Betty Williams.

Contents

The most popular longhair in the world has long been the Persian. The variety of colors and affectionate, winning nature of these cats make them second to none among purebred cats. Owners, Charles A. and Susan P. Heitman-Helmke.

I Bought Me A Cat

I bought me a cat.
My cat pleased me.
I fed my cat under yonder tree.
My cat said 'Fiddle-Eye-Fee.'

Only daffy happy cats mutter "Fiddle-Eye-Fee." If buying and caring for a cat could be so easy!

The uniqueness of every cat's *person*ality makes the selection of one breed over another a matter of esthetic preference, color prejudice, and possibly a mouse-sized need for utility. The feline is not predictable—no two cats are ever alike, regardless of breed status, color, sex, age, or political affiliation.

If you grew up with a tabby, you likely will continue to enjoy keeping a tabby in tandem; if mom only likes white cats, a colored kitten may not fill the bill. In choosing a pet dog, there are1,000,001 considerations: size, function, temperament, abilities, indoor/outdoor adaptability, etc. Cats are more simple. There are no encyclopedias geared towards choosing a cat with the right temperament to stop an intruder, pull a sled, chase a fallen

Cats of a feather.... This two-stepping Colorpoint Shorthair has much to recommend his creativity and color coordination. Owner,Cher Kelly.

pheasant, or mouth a menacing mink from a stream. Cats will do as cats will do. Cats will gladly disdain an intruder, but will not attempt to forcefully do *anything*; cats often like Huskies since they are snugglesome; cats will oblige, with minimal objection, to torment a half-dying ground bird, though they'd prefer to de-flight

celebrities, and clergy—the Mayflower, Titanic, and lots of HMS's have employed cats.

Most people who love cats are basically indiscriminate about the cat they choose. Most cats pretty much look like cats. Since man has been completely unsuccessful (or nearly so) in molding the cat's spirit into a

Exercise is an important component in the life of a house cat. This Somali is doing his morning stretching. Owner, Carolyn S. Goldberg.

the fowl themselves; and cats, unless they're Turkish, don't do water.

Some cats will chase mice— even rats—preferably mice (rats are bigger and seem to see death coming and fight like mad). If you need a good mouser, the cat has an impressive track record: they've even done it for royalty,

desirable temperament—which is to say bred-for predictable tendencies—most any cat makes a good choice. Likewise, man has not tampered with the near-perfect feline physique: some bodies are longish, others cobbyish, and others in-betweenish.

Therefore, *The Right Cat for Me* ideally could end right here!

However, since there were so many great photographs available, and since all cats are pretty to look at, we'll continue to ponder this question for a few more moments or about a hundred or more pages—let's not feel rushed. Cats never make hasty decisions but more often decide not to decide . . . or choose to forget the question.

Few feats escape the Exotic Shorthair. This super cat is owned by Mr. and Mme. Prin.

Cat breeds can be divided into two different camps: longhaired breeds and shorthaired breeds. The former group is dominated by the fabulous Persian and the other long-furred people of the feline community. Longhairs are, in general, infinitely regal and surprisingly elegant despite the many inches of fluff and fur they tote about. These cats prove more similar in type than do the shorthaired breeds. The shorthaired breeds are more diverse and consist of the basic domestic shorthairs, namely American Shorthairs and British Shorthairs—Of course most

European nations have their own equivalent to these cats and the longer bodied, lithe breeds of the Orient. Among the most prominent shorthaired breeds are the Siamese and Abyssinian, two breeds which are fundamental to the cat world and from which many

Every European nation has its equivalent of our domestic shorthair breeds. This is the European Shorthair, a most unexaggerated and sensible citizen from the Continent.

other breeds descend or sprout, especially the family of Oriental shorthaired breeds. Generally all these shorthaired breeds are sleek, graceful and mysterious, not to mention more utilitarian.

The question of color, again, is one that often persuades buyers to get fussy. Even simple folk who once were satisfied with a gray cat are slurped into the spinning color kaleidoscope and suddenly *prefer* richer tones of honey, ermine and champagne. The cat's color possibilities are endless, due to its kinky genetics and breeders of purebred cats thrive on this, as well as do battle.

Traditions are largely responsible for the color of the different breeds—some breeds are defined merely by a color dissension, such as the Colorpoint Shorthair. Case in point, although an avant-garde fancier in Los Angeles is happily spending his days developing a fuchsia-pointed Siamese, traditional fanciers will still only accept the four "original" colors. The authors would love to see a fluorescent fuchsia cat, since we've already found a handsome lavender one! Of course, our desire for a true green cat were not abated in the deceivingly named Chartreux (which is blue-gray, not liquor

The Chartreux of France is celebrated for his rich blue-gray coat and beautiful golden-copper eyes. The breed is never found in green. Owner, Emily Orca Starbuck.

green). Incidentally the Russian Blue is aptly named and doesn't promise "blue skies" but more realistically the gray skies that any Russian play guarantees (apologies to Irving, Ira and Anton!).

Why not A.O.C. (that's "Any Old Cat")? We're still considering color. If you have the slightest inkling about the cat's inking (color), A.O.C. may not meet your needs. Haphazard matings in alleyways of multicolored cats frequently result in some eye-soring patterns and combos.

Admittedly, cats, who can also see and discern color, have better reasons for disliking humans than humans do for disliking cats—since men can never escape our "color" vision. Ironically, cats exhibit good judgment in summing up the humans they meet and, in a different world, would excel in choosing *The Right Human For Me* (and probably wouldn't need a book!).

Cats would likely be even more successful in categorizing humans as possible owners, much the way the authors have broken this text down into chapters. In Chapter One, "Why *Not* To Buy a Human?", the author cat would point out man's inescapable tragic flaws: he is fundamentally dumb, too moody, moves around too much, never stops fussing, and is never content with the way things are. In Chapter Two, "A.D.H." (that is, "Another Dumb *Homo sapien*"), the cat would determine that man cannot be depended on for making decisions, is constantly uttering "why" and keeps reading books about cat breeds. In chapters Three and Four, "Worthy Cat Owners" and "Lowlife, Dog-owning Yardbirds To Avoid," the cat could divide humans into two basic camps (the latter a concentration camp) and identify all the necessary qualities of a worthy cat owner.

Humans must keep in mind that, while cats are pretty easy to keep, they may not be easy to live with. Cats are *in*: *in*dulgent, and *in*telligent, and

There's no joshing the Oriental Shorthair.

The longhaired Himalayan wonder known as Samson is the indulgent but loving companion of Doris De Prisco.

*in*stinctual. They are extremely sensitive and sensible, not to mention sensual. Cats don't need both eyes to see everything. In deference to the vast number of homeless cats in the world, cat adopters (prospective owners) must determine if they are cat-owning material.

Cat owners characteristically are open-minded and respectful individuals—sensitive to the delicate balance of nature and sanity, to the needs of fellow creatures, to the joys of free thought and unprejudiced views. Cat owners, nevertheless, are discriminate and discerning, eternally curious, camouflaging their indecisiveness with mood swings and varying occupations. These conscientious, caring folk are not molders or trainers—they understand the feline's need to develop his own personality traits, to find his niche in the home routine, and to feel secure in his role as a cat.

No breed of cat can compete with the luxuriant coat of the Classic Brown Tabby Persian. Owner, H. Keith McDaniel.

The Persian breed is divided only by color. Persians can be solid colors, such as this beautiful White owned by Sally K. Robinson, or bicolored, patterned, pointed or shaded.

Persian

The remarkable Eastern longhaired purebred known as the Persian, and sometimes simply as the Longhair in Britain, plausibly results from the early imported cats brought to the Continent by Pietro Valla in the latter half of the sixteenth century. Historical accounts validate Valla's journey, and we are quite sure that he brought with him densely furred Eastern cats. These cats raised the furry eyebrows of the Europeans, and this exotic import stole the attention from other longhaired cats already living on the Continent. The Angoras of Turkey, long and silky in coat, were replaced by the more densely furred Persians.

The dense coat of the Persian became the focus of European breeders and much interbreeding of the Angora cats and the newly imported Persians took place. Realistically, it is difficult to imagine too much planned breeding taking place by cat keepers in the 1500s, though this series of events is commonly recorded in recounting the Persian's evolution and development. We imagine that the imported cats of Valla had coats which cannot possibly compete with the luxuriant coats of today's Persian breed. Additionally, the puggy face of the breed today was bred for at some much later point. The breed experienced

The Black Persian's deep copper eyes add to his fancy appeal. Owner, Laura Donaghue.

great alterations in conformation and body structure over the centuries. Certain early specimens had very pronounced muzzles, others were rather flat faced, etc. Coat type also varied, with woolliness being common—regardless, these cats always had a lot of coat.

When this breed caught on in Britain, it was the favored child of the cat fancy, frequently longhaired darling meandered on the scene. England has never strayed from the Longhair, not even with the dramatic entrance of the Siamese.

The Persian has long reigned as the principal force in the cat world. Not only has the breed kept the heart and eye of the fancy since the genesis of cat shows but it also has been a major contributor to the

Silver Tabby Persian kitten owned by Mr. and Mme. Prin.

swiping First Place in cat competitions, not too unlike these beauties do today! The British Shorthair had just about gotten a paw pad of acceptance and favor by the time this development of other breeds. Ironically, the Persian was the main contributing factor to the revival of today's Turkish Angora breed, a breed which generations ago it outshined and

The Cream Persian is a solid-colored cat that derives from the Orange Persian; it is a variety that is particularly difficult to breed. Owners, Kathy Young and Sharon Pinkerton.

The Bicolor Persian in blue and white ranks among the most attractive Persian patterns. Owners, Charles and Susan Helmke.

forced into oblivion. Breeders today recognize the sublimity of the Persian's purity and have no other choice when trying to augment a breed's coat quality.

As a house cat, the Persian has also usurped a permanent pedestal, window, and anywhere else it decides to prop its luxurious self. These cats require a great deal of attention for grooming and general upkeep. Daily brushing helps to avoid matting, which is a common problem with the breed. Don't overbrush the Persian or it may become bald from your good-intentioned zeal. The personality of the breed can be accurately described as aloof with sporadic outpourings of purring affection. These are delicate, gentle-voiced cats that strive on a peaceful home setting and a strong paw on what goes on. Some owners claim that the Persian is the most affectionate of all cats, though more commonly these cats prefer independence to constant cooing and cuddling. Extremely intelligent and discerning, the Persian is an astoundingly adaptable and tolerant soul that defies description. Having been bred selectively for generations as companion animals, the Persian relates better to the concept of domestication than do most other homebound cats. Generally these are low-key companions that are pleased to be catered to indoors, though an afternoon stroll through the garden with a family member can be a rewarding diversion for the Persian.

The appearance of today's Persian is cobby with a low-set and massive body, never coarse. The body is well muscled with a level back. The legs are short and thick, the forelegs must be straight. The paws are round and firm, sort of big with well carried toes. The Persian's head is broad and perfectly round. The nose, with a notable break, is rather pug-like, snubby and short. Ears tilt forward with a rounded tip. Eyes are large, round and most prominent. The Persian coat is dense, thick, and flowing, most off-standing. The entire body is heavily coated with an enormous ruff, full brush and tufts on the ears and toes.

As with the British Shorthair, the British club regards each color of the Longhair as an individual breed. The following colors (breeds) are recognized in England and America as well. Of course, American clubs regard all these colors merely as varieties of the Persian breed.

The Blue Persian has large copper eyes and has long been a highly regarded variety. Owner, Carol Fogarty.

A pair of Persians, solid and bicolored. The Bicolor is the red and white combination.

BLACK PERSIAN

As coal shimmers, so should the coat of the Black Persian; every hair is black without a single trace of white or rustiness. By eight months, the kitten will be pure solid black. The eyes of the Black Persian are deep orange or brilliant copper in color. The paw pads ideally are black, though sometimes they are brown. The nose pad is black.

WHITE PERSIAN

A classic color for the Longhair, the White has either blue, orange or odd eyes. Deafness may occur in the blue-eyed cat, and sometimes in the odd eye as well. Pads are pink.

CREAM PERSIAN

Originally considered an Orange-gone bad, the Cream Persian is a fairly recent addition to the Persian lines and was developed from off-white cats. Cream-colored cats were dismissed commonly by British fanciers, mostly out of the commonness of the color as well as frustrations, as the color is difficult to breed for intentionally. The eyes are rich copper in color and the paw and nose pads are pink.

BLUE PERSIAN

Black and White Persians were used to develop the Blue Persian, a distinctive cat which

The Red Persian may appear solid or in a tabby pattern. Owners, Anthony and Sharon Pestano.

has been highly regarded since the early 1900s in England, and which was a favorite of Queen Victoria. This is essentially a diluted black with brilliant copper eyes and blue pads.

RED PERSIAN

The Red Persian is a deep orange-red in color with copper eyes and brick-red pads. Often Red Tabbies and Peke-faced Reds are regarded as Red Persians, but this point is the cause for much debate in the cat world.

BLUE-CREAM PERSIAN

A wondrous mixture of pale cream and blues distinguishes this Longhair. Americans prefer a blue-cream that exhibits more clearly defined patches, while the English are not as selective in this regard. Nose and paw pads are blue.

The Blue-Cream Persian, like the Red, has deep copper eyes.

The Bicolor Persian has a solid white coat evenly marked with a another color. This Bicolor is black and white.

The Chinchilla Persian has an attractive, unique coat tinged in silver. Owner, Preston Dess.

CHINCHILLA PERSIAN

Sometimes regarded as the Shaded Silver, the Chinchilla Persian has a white ground color with a silver residue throughout. The eyes are the color of emeralds or aqua. The nose is pink and paw pads are black.

CAMEO PERSIAN

In a variety of colors and patterns, the Cameo turns heads from the outer color's contrasting with the pure white undercoat. Varieties accepted for the Cameo are Red Shell, Red Shaded, Red Smoke; Cream Shell, Cream Shaded, Cream Smoke, Blue-Cream; Tortie and Tabby. These colors vary in the amount of tipping; all varieties have copper eyes.

SMOKE PERSIAN

These orange-eyed beauties are tipped in black or blue in Britain; in the U.S., cats can also be tortie, lilac, chocolate and blue-cream. The cats' distinctive white undercoat contrasts with the outer color.

BICOLOR PERSIAN

Evenly distributed patches against a pure white background, the Bicolor can be marked in red, blue, black, lilac or cream. The Van Bicolor, promoted in the States, is a Persian whose markings are similar to the Turkish Van, that is, pure white body with patches on head and tail. Eyes are orange or copper in all varieties. Pads are pink.

Bicolor Persian owned by Ali Kretschmar.

TABBY PERSIAN

The tabby pattern occurs more commonly in the shorthaired breeds, though Persians of these patterns do exist. Among the accepted Tabbies are the Red, Brown, Silver, Blue, Cream, Cameo, Patched (sometimes called Torbie), Chocolate, and Lilac. As in the shorthaired breeds, the patterns can be either classic or mackerel. Eyes are copper, orange or hazel. Torbies occur in silver, brown or blue mixed with markings of red and/or cream.

The Calico Persian is called Tortoiseshell and White in England. Regardless of its name, it is an enchanting feline. Owner, Joan A. Duca.

Red Tabby is a striking pattern in a longhaired cat like these Persians. Owners, Anthony and Sharon Preston.

TORTOISESHELL PERSIAN

Due to the sex-linked gene of the Tortie, this breed is virtually always female, making breeding difficult to overcome. Shell and Shaded varieties are known. Shadeds in England are called Cameo. American clubs requires that a Tortie Persian have clear unbrindled patches of red and cream. The eyes are copper or orange. Pads on the paws are black or pink.

CALICO PERSIAN

The British do not recognize the Calico coloration and label it a Tortoiseshell and White. The color of the Calico is white with patches of blue and cream or black and red on the upper body of the cat (i.e., head, back and tail). The patches are clear and unbrindled.

COLORPOINT PERSIAN

This color variety was established by crossing the Persian to the Siamese. From the Siamese, the Colorpoint acquired its bright sapphire-blue eyes and its color points. Originally the Colorpoint, more frequently called the Himalayan, occurred only in the four traditional Siamese points. Today, in addition to the traditional seal, lilac, chocolate and blue, Colorpoints can be seen in flame, cream, tortie, blue-cream, lilac-cream, chocolate-tortie, and lynx. The undercoat is always a soft warm color, and the points maintained on the face, tail, and paws.

Above: *The Colorpoint Persian, commonly loved as the Himalayan, ranks among the most popular of the Longhairs.* **Below:** *Tortoiseshell Persian owned by Charles and Susan Helmke.*

Dilute Calico Persian owned by Victoria Marant.

Tabby point Persian owned by Elizabeth Stamper. The Persian has contributed blood to more longhairs than any other purebred.

The Norwegian Forest Cat is a rugged individualist, complete with a long thick coat and hearty instincts. Owner, Penny M. Kopf.

Longhairs

Primped and polished, the longhairs are the most impressive of all cats, truly the lords of the modern jungle. They come from the Orient, the Middle East, from Europe and America. They have lured and allured, captured and captivated.

Longhaired cats have long existed in most parts of the world, and for many years, particularly in the West, their innate beauty was long unappreciated. It was not until the Persian made his debut in Great Britain that the English-speaking world realized what a cat they had in their cap. The popularity of the Persian paved the way for other longhairs, and today the longhaired breeds are maintained and furthered by some of the most dedicated and enthusiastic of all feline fraternities.

Many of these longhairs are offspring of a shorthaired 'parent' breed—the Oriental Longhair and Longhair Scottish Fold, the Cymric and Somali, for example. These cats are typically the products of genetic mutations that occurred in the parent breed and, because of the strong appeal of a luxurious long coat, were fostered by captivated fanciers. Some

The fabulous Somali offers the charm, elegance and grace of the Abyssinian in a long coat. Owner, Karen E. Leblanc.

The Persian, a cat of perfection for hundreds of years, nevertheless gets better and better: new colors, richer hues and remarkable conformation, all graced with a lovely temperament. Owner, Elizabeth Stamper.

longhairs are hybrids, typically Persian or Siamese crosses—and, in the case of the Himalayan, a Persian and Siamese cross. These cats can be called the products of popularity: always attempting to turn good to better, breeders blend genes to create new colors, new coats, new cats. Often these breeds display the best of both parent breeds and make nice choices as pets and showmen. Breeds such as the Maine Coon, Norwegian Forest Cat, and the two Turks are purebreds, meaning that little to no infusion of other breeds has occurred in many years. These

breeds are uniquely their own and, in addition to their unique characters and conformation, offer owners a long and interesting history to investigate—it is a nice pastime for the Norwegian Forest Cat owner to page through ancient Norse fables in search of references to his breed.

Perhaps the two most important considerations for the potential longhair owner are that longhairs are typically slow to mature, not attaining full adult conformation until two to three years of age, and that longhairs invariably require more grooming than

The ancestors of the Turkish Angora predate the cat we know as the Persian. These lovely white cats were overcome by the Persian's popularity when that breed was first introduced to Europe. They have long coats that are not as thick and luxurious as the Persian's. Owner, B. Tannes.

their shorthaired cousins. There are two breeds, the Balinese and Javanese, which are single-coated longhairs, meaning that they have no undercoats. If one strongly desires a longhair but is hesitant about excessive grooming, these two breeds should be considered, provided one appreciates the foreign-type conformation. If primping and patience are no problem, then any one of these beautiful felines can make the perfect cat for the right owner.

AMERICAN CURL

The American Curl unfurls distinct ears that set it apart from all other cat breeds. The Curl can be a good choice of cat for the breeder-owner who has at least some knowledge of genetics and genetic mutations. This basic knowledge is requisite because of the relative newness of the breed. While no serious abnormalities as a result of this mutation have yet occurred, possibilities still exist, particularly if inexperienced breeders attempt to satisfy the popular demand.

The ears resulted from a natural genetic mutation and

The American Curl is surely the cutest mutant to enter the cat fancy in ages. Owner, Caroline Scott.

were first displayed by a longhaired black California stray named Shulamith, who was found by Joe and Grace Ruga outside their West Coast home and served as the single foundation cat for this new breed. Because the curled ears are dominant over regular ears, only one of a mating pair need possess the curl gene. This dominance has helped considerably in the breed's introduction to the cat world. First appearing in 1981, the Curl was granted full recognition by the American registry T.I.C.A. in 1986.

The American Curl is a lively, interesting cat who continuously wins new fanciers with his unique appearance and good-natured character, which is fully and "unmutatedly" feline. In general appearance he is a medium-sized, well-balanced, rather slender cat, said to be of a "semi-foreign" type. Two coat types occur, a medium-long and a longer. Coat is silky in texture and lies flat to the body. In the longer variety, undercoat is minimal. His distinctively curled ears are set at the corners of the head, carried erect and open, curving in a gentle curl back from the face, pointing toward the center of the back of the head. It is a disqualification in the breed if the tip of the ear should touch the back of the ear or the head.

The unique ear construction of the American Curl, complemented by his outgoing, good-natured personality, wins new Curl converts on a daily basis. Owner, Caroline Scott.

BALINESE

With the exception of his long luxurious coat, the Balinese is Siamese through and through, and offers Siamese fanciers the option of owning that wondrous cat in an altogether different vestige. Even the colorpoints of the breed are the same— is slender and lithe, with quality musculature. The Bali character denotes intelligence, inquisitiveness, and demonstrative affection. Like the Siamese, the breed is known for its vocalizations and penetrating expressions. Differing from other longhairs,

The beauty and personality of the Siamese in a long coat make the Balinese irresistible to any true cat lover. Balinese are among the most affectionate and intelligent cats in the world. Owner, M. Ferenczi.

pointed in either seal, blue, chocolate, or lilac, each with the base coat of its respective Siamese counterpart. General conformation is classically Siamese: head is a long, tapering wedge; ears are large; eyes, almond-shaped and slanting towards the nose. Body the Balinese has a single coat, which means no undercoat and, necessarily, easier grooming, no matting and less shedding than the double-coated longhairs. "Longhair Siamese" in other than the four classic colorpoints are called Javanese.

The Sacred Cat of Burma, the Birman is an ancient breed of great purity and nobility. Owners, Rita Rechsteiner and Gayle Geering, DVM.

BIRMAN

The Birman is adorned with a long silky coat, attractively colorpointed, with white "mittens." Owing to these points, as well as the well-rounded head, full cheeks, thick-set legs, and long coat, one might, at first glance, suspect that the breed is a cross between the Persian and Siamese. However, the Birman is believed to be a purebred whose history and evolution are lost to time and the terrain of Burma and Tibet—and outcrosses to Siamese and Persians are strictly forbidden. Like the ancient priests who

Hallmarks of the Birman breed are its unique violet eyes and white mittens. Owner, Paula Boroff.

cultivated the early breed, the Birman possesses a character which is placid and scholarly; yet, owing to its feline heritage, the Birman has moments of intense activity and great inquisitiveness. Available colorpoints are the same as the Siamese, namely seal, blue, chocolate, and lilac. Juveniles typically display a lighter variation of color until maturity. Eye color tends toward violet, or deepish blue. In all, the Birman is an exceedingly attractive cat, with much to recommend it to potential owners.

CYMRIC

The tailless Cymric traces directly to a spontaneous mutation that occurred in the Manx breed. As best as can be determined, no outcrosses were involved in the breed's creation, but outcrossing, including to the Manx, is necessary for the preservation of the Cymric. Excepting the coat, which is medium in length, double, and very profuse, the breed demonstrates Manx conformation: basically compact, sturdy, and well balanced. The degree of taillessness can vary and is broken down into four categories: 1. Rumpy-riser, having a few vertebrae; 2. Stumpy, having longer, often kinked or deformed tail; 3. Longie, having tail shorter than full length but longer than other Manx types; and 4. Absolute, having no tail at all. As for the Manx, absolute taillessness is most desired. Additionally, the Cymric is affected by the same potential genetic abnormalities, prenatal deaths and other problems that occur in the Manx, and owners must choose carefully, purchasing only a cat of quality and responsible breeding. The Cymric can be just about any color or combination of colors, except chocolate, lavender, or Himalayan pattern.

EXOTIC LONGHAIR

Recognized only in Canada, the Exotic Longhair is the longhaired variety of the more common Exotic Shorthair, which was created by crossing Persians and American Shorthairs. The Exotic Longhair demonstrates all the qualities of the Persian, except that it may also occur in American Shorthair and Himalayan colors. Fanciers assert the breed's personality represents the ideal blend of both the Persian and Shorthair, and outcrosses to both still occur.

The tailless Cymric descends from the cats from the Isle of Man, the Manx, who are also tailless but shortcoated. Owner, Donna Chandler.

The Himalayan has overcome its hybrid status into a fully recognized pure breed unto itself. Though not recognized by some registries and shown in the Persian classes, the Himalayan has a strong and dedicated following. Owner, Elizabeth Stamper.

HIMALAYAN

The popular and pleasing Himalayan is a hybrid created by crossing the Persian with the Siamese to attain the latter's colorpoints. These crosses are known to have occurred as long ago as the 1920s. Since that time, breeders have carefully selected to eliminate all Siamese qualities except the desired colorpoints, and the breed today is commonly labeled the Colorpoint Persian or Colorpoint Longhair and registered as a Persian— particularly in Great Britain. Today the Himalayan is Persian in everything but color, which can be pointed in seal, blue, chocolate, lilac, red tortie, cream, blue cream, lilac, lilac cream, chocolate tortie, tabby lynx, as well as self colors and bicolors. Bred to the highest of standards for decades, the Himalayan fits perfectly into many cat-loving households. The breed is inquisitive, lively, and loving, and specimens are not hard to come by, though quality specimens can command a high price. Additionally, the luxurious coat requires daily attention.

JAVANESE

The Javanese, like his close cousin, the Balinese, differs from the Siamese only in coat length. While the Balinese occurs in the four traditional Siamese points, the Javanese offers nearly 20 possible colorpoints that include all those of the Colorpoint Shorthair, the breed's shorthaired counterpart. His general conformation clearly says 'Siamese.' The long, tapering wedge of the head; large, ears; and slanted, almond-shaped eyes are all classic features. Body is slender and lithe, solid and elegantly balanced. Intelligence, curiosity, extroversion, and affection are all standard in the Javanese character. Versatile with his voice and clear with his expectations, the Javanese makes a most interesting and companionable feline. Differing from other longhairs, the medium-length Javanese coat has no undercoat and therefore makes for easier grooming and less shedding than the other longhairs.

The Javanese is endowed with the Siamese cat's affectionate nature and inimitable animation. Owner, Margaret Lowther.

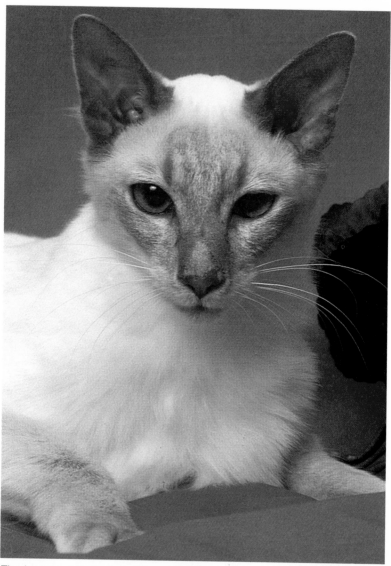

The Javanese belongs to the Siamese family of cats, from whom it differs only in coat length. These are graceful, intelligent felines in a striking array of colorpoints. Owner, Heather Kalt.

The Longhair Scottish Fold is a modern variation of the Scottish Fold, a cat that has been popular for generations. Like its progenitor, the breed is unique for its ear set. Owners, Gary and Diane Finch-Smith.

KASHMIR

Recognized only in Canada, the Kashmir is essentially a self-colored Himalayan in lilac (a frosty gray with pinkish tone) or chocolate (a warm rich chocolate). These colors are not recognized for either the Himalayan or Persian by certain organizations and thus serve as the breed's stamp of uniqueness. In all other qualities, the Kashmir is Persian (or Himalayan).

LONGHAIR SCOTTISH FOLD

The Longhair Scottish Fold is the longhaired variety of the Scottish Fold, a breed unique for its distinctly folded ears. Unlike some other longhaired varieties, the Longhair Scottish Fold, to the best of our knowledge, was not created by any outcrosses. It is reported that longhairs simply occurred in shorthaired litters, which is not surprising considering the farm-cat ancestry of the Fold breed. These longhairs have been carefully bred, and today the lucky cat world has a Scottish Fold in a long coat. In all other qualities, the breed is certainly Scottish Fold, having the same general appearance: a medium-sized, well-rounded body—never cobby or

Above: *The Longhair Scottish Fold has a plush, thick coat comparable to the hardiest outdoor cat. Owners, Gary and Diane Finch-Smith.* Below: *The Longhair Scottish Fold comes in a wide array of colors and patterns. This young cat reveals his van-patterned coat. Owners, Gary and Diane Finch-Smith.*

coarse—with a broad, round head; round, well-padded feet; and legs which give the appearance of shortness. Tail length can vary from medium to long, with longer and more tapering preferred. Nearly all colors and combinations are perfectly fine. Coat is semi-long, profuse, and flowing. In character, the breed should be considered a domestic or British Shorthair. Because of the mutation, breeding should be left to the experts.

MAINE COON

No breed historian can state with any certainty whence the Maine Coon came. What is known is that this large, muscular, abundantly coated

The tabby and white patterns in the Maine Coon are among the most popular, though the breed has been loved in solid coats for generations. Owners, Richard and Meryle Weiss.

breed was developed (or evolved) in North America. Though theories set the Maine Coon's first American paw prints back to the Vikings and even before, the most likely scenario involves domestic shorthairs brought by settlers in the 1600s. The breed today is renowned for its substance and stout character. He is a large cat, with broad, well-adorned chest and good musculature; his head is rather long with sizable ears. The Maine Coon's coat is long and flowing, thick and shaggy, though not given to matting. The coat sheds seasonally. Eyes are large, set wide apart, and slant slightly toward the outer base of the ear. Eye color varies in accordance with the coat colors, which are many and commonly divided into the following categories: solids, tabbies, tabbies with white, partis, and smokes. These cats are given to independence—which does not exclude the right to bestow affection—and require considerable outlets to expend their energy and satisfy their curiosity. Along with the American and British Shorthair, the breed is perhaps the finest of all purebred hunters and enjoys the great outdoors.

A solid-colored Maine Coon in peak form. This cat won Best Cat at the 1994 Madison Square Garden Cat Show. Owners, Thom and Suzanne Shambaugh.

Silver tabby and white Maine Coon owned by Richard and Meryle Weiss.

Silver mackerel tabby Maine Coon owned by Evelyn Rae Powers.

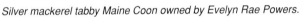

The profusely coated Norwegian Forest Cats are among the hardiest of all purebred cats, having derived from the sturdy outdoor cats of the Scandinavian countries. Owner, Penny M. Koft.

NORWEGIAN FOREST CAT

The Norwegian Forest Cat, or Norsk Skaukatt, is an ancient breed native to Scandinavia. References can be found in old Norse fables, and it is believed that these cats developed for centuries largely without selective breeding by man. Like the Maine Coon, to which breed the Forest Cat has been suggested as a contributor, the Norwegian Forest offers potential owners a cat of great substance and instinct. He is a large cat, with heavy bone and overall powerful appearance. Head is triangular, with medium-large ears and large, almond-shaped eyes. Tail is long and flowing, ideally of equal length to the body. Coat is long, smooth, soft and double, with oily (water-repellent) guard hairs throughout and a profuse ruff around the neck. Except for colorpoints, all colors and combinations of colors are perfectly acceptable in the breed. The long coat sheds seasonally. The breed's popularity outside its homeland is relatively low, but keen fanciers maintain the breed. A Norwegian Forest can be acquired without excessive effort. The reason for the breed's relative lack of popularity is simply that other rugged longhairs (e.g., the Maine Coon) are not as uncommon.

The Norwegian Forest Cat's head is triangular with medium-large ears. His expression is keen and intelligent. Owner, Dawn M. Shiley.

The neck ruff of the Norwegian Forest Cat gives the breed a distinctive appearance. Owner, Penny M. Koft.

The Norwegian Forest Cat can be seen in solid colors, like this black and blue-gray (above), as well as traditional tabby patterns, like the brown tabby (below). Owners, Dawn M. Shiley and Bob and Lisa Thaler.

ORIENTAL LONGHAIR

The Oriental Longhair can be described as the longhaired counterpart to the Oriental Shorthair. The breed was likely created by crossing the Shorthair to the Persian or Himalayan to achieve the desired long coat. Selective breeding eliminated all "non-Siamese" qualities, and the Oriental Longhair today is just that—a cat with a distinctly Oriental appearance and semi-long coat. Color, as for the Shorthair, can be various solids, shadeds, tortoiseshells, smokes, and tabbies—indeed a myriad of possibilities. Essentially, the breed offers cat lovers the opportunity to enjoy the Oriental in a long coat and wide range of colors.

RAGDOLL

The Ragdoll is so named because of its propensity to "go limp" when handled. Theories (some most unscientific) differ regarding the development of this characteristic, and the most scientific refer to a similar trait developed in laboratory mice. But there is much more to the Ragdoll, as these are large, full-bodied cats of affectionate character and attractive coloration. Slow to

A unique package of sleekness and grace in a long silky coat, the Oriental Longhair is an unbeatable combination.

The Ragdoll is an uncommon longhair with uncommonly beautiful blue eyes. Owners, Kim Brantley and Bob Balas.

The Ragdoll kitten is born solid white and attains its adult markings with age. This adorable doll is owned by Susan Bugdin.

Ragdolls come in an astonishing array of colors and patterns, from classic Siamese points to mittened-particolors to vibrant solids with shadings. Owners, Kim Brantley and Bob Balas.

mature, the substantial Ragdoll does not reach its full-grown, solidly muscled size until about four years of age. Kittens are born white and do not attain full adult coloration until about two years of age. Coat color can be divided into three categories: Solid, a solid base, with lighter shading to darker points on face, feet, and tail; Particolor-mitted, darker points, with white stripe on body, and white mittens on front and back feet; and Bi-color, white chest, stomach, and all four legs, with points on ears, mask, and tail. The Ragdoll is registered by several cat associations, but currently there is some dispute between founder Ann Baker and other breeders—of course, it is not necessary for potential owners to take sides.

The Somali is a talented, affectionate offspring of the ever-popular Aby. Owner, Patricia A. Freberg.

Somalis make expressive, entertaining pets; they are breathtakingly elegant and naturally beautiful cats. Owner, Karen E. Leblanc.

SOMALI

According to the best of records, the Somali is simply the longhaired version of the Abyssinian which was developed by a spontaneous mutation that occurred in American-bred cats. The fur is longest on the tail; the ears are tufted, and the cheeks, well adorned. The hair on the body is medium in length, only slightly longer than that of the Aby. While his appearance is basically Abyssinian, the mutation for long hair has produced a more rounded appearance, primarily because longer hair tends to soften curves. Color, as for the Aby, can be ruddy (orange brown, ticked with two or three bands), sorrel (warm cinnamon, ticked with chocolate brown), blue (warm, soft blue-gray, ticked with deeper blue), or fawn (warm pinkish buff, ticked with deeper shade of pinkish buff). Eye color can be gold, copper, green, or hazel. The Somali has gained recognition by several major registries and maintains a strong though not very large following both in the U.S. and Europe. He is a delightful cat with true Aby character.

TURKISH ANGORA

Also known simply as Angora, this ancient breed of Asian cat is purported to be the forebear of the ever-popular Persian. The Angora is a medium to small cat, with long svelte features and an overall graceful appearance. Head is with a silk-like sheen. Only a slight undercoat is present, making grooming easier and shedding less a concern. The breed occurs in 12 attractive colors, including solids, smokes, tabbies, and torties. Eye color is typically amber, but whites have blue or odd

While white Turkish Angoras have a certain classic, traditional appeal, the breed comes in 12 attractive colors and patterns. Owner, M. Clemensat.

wedge-shaped, with high-set tufted ears and large almond-shaped eyes that slant slightly upward. Like other longhairs, the breed is slow to mature, not reaching its majestic adulthood until about two years of age. The distinctive Angora coat is semi-long, with an abundant ruff around the neck. Its texture is very fine, eyes, and silvers and goldens have green eyes. The Turkish Angora is perhaps the ideal cat for the longhair fancier who prefers a characteristically mellow, docile cat, one not given to over-excitability and yet very affectionate. Like its likely kinsman, the Turkish Van, the Angora possesses a certain affinity for water.

The Turkish Angora is an active and stylish indoor cat. Owner, M. Clemensat.

The Turkish Van, traditionally seen in the van pattern— white with auburn—can also be seen in blacks, blues, torties and torbies. Owner, B. Tannes.

TURKISH VAN

Nicknamed the swimming cat for its proclivity to take to water, the Turkish Van is among the oldest of all cat breeds. The Van is a semi-longhaired white cat with distinct markings and full ruff development in males. A solid and substantial cat, the Van's body is long, broad and muscular. The head tapers as a wedge, with wide-set ears that are feathered internally and eyes that vary from almond-shaped to almost round, typically set straight. The classic van pattern occurs as red (auburn) markings on a pure white base; these markings create a blazed head patch and rump patch extending to the tip of the tail,

This kitten possesses the classic van pattern. Owner, Frank A. Szablowski.

Turkish Vans make delightful, independent companions with much personality and smarts. Owner, B. Tannes.

with one or more random spots permitted on the upper body, flanks, and outside of legs to the ankles. Other colors do occur, including cream and white, black and white, blue and white, and various torties and torbies. The Turkish Vans are typically very well-behaved companions, long schooled in domesticity. They are intelligent and quite intrepid. While exercise and diversion are musts, little in the way of special demands are asked by these easygoing longhairs.

American through and through, this cat is full of spunk, independence and good will. Owner, Paul W. Jurkowski.

American Shorthair

Native American Indians and their flea-ridden pariah dogs did not benefit from the pesticidal instincts of the newly immigrated shorthaired cats. The pilgrims who came to America naturally brought along the family cat, who was not only a clean cabin mate but also a hardy rat and mouse exterminator. The cat's natural desire to snag a passing rodent attracted man's attention for centuries and the industrious feline dearly regarded the acquaintanceship of its human admirers. Today's purebred American Shorthair derives from these European cats who arrived in North America around 1620. Nevertheless, these cats bred and interbred for nearly the next three centuries without humans giving them a second thought. Before Americans (and their cross-Atlantic British counterparts) began to revere their native street cats, they were coddling and grooming imported Longhairs, today's Persians and Angoras. The average shorthair was effective as a hunter and ever so self-sufficient, hardly amenable to much cooing from the human species. Thus, when people became interested in breeding cats and exhibiting cats, imported Longhairs and other exotics took centerstage—and the tough, stout-hearted alley cat was all too glad.

Silver Classic Tabby American Shorthair owned by Elaine F. Martin.

This free-spirited street life, however, would not persist too much longer, and Americans began to consider the virtues of these lithe and athletic little knock-about clowns. The breed standard for the American Shorthair did not originate as a description of one passing or fox-trotting alley cat. The ideal conformation of the cat derives from what would be the "perfect" working cat, which the American Shorthair, without coincidence, happens to be. Through the centuries, these cats adapted to a varied environment, much like the settlers who kept them: this was a rugged, healthy and autonomous kitty. Thus the standard for the American Shorthair, which the original fanciers began to follow, emphasized the natural and unexaggerated appearance of the "breed." Today's breed continues to emulate the free spirit, autonomy and strong work ethic of its American founding fathers.

Cat lovers today may question the value of purchasing a purebred cat that is intentionally geared to look like just "any old cat," a regular "tom" about town. Although American

White American Shorthairs make grand show cats, since mousing and fussing with the daily chores are no longer priorities. Owner, Margot Mellies.

Common sense and workmanlike intelligence characterize the American Shorthair breed. Owner, Elaine F. Martin.

fanciers believe that the American Shorthair looks distinctively purebred, less informed cat purchasers may not notice without being told. The advantages of owning a purebred American Shorthair are not difficult to enumerate.

The earliest attempts of breeders focused on fixing the color varieties that existed and reproducing them with consistency. As a result, the American Shorthair in every coat possibility is a genetically sound and structurally ideal feline. Pedigrees, which result from registering cats so that parentages are known, are also a clear advantage so that any potential problems can be traced and thereby eliminated.

Comparing this American purebred to its British cousin, one will find that the American Shorthair is a more massive and strongly built animal whose face is somewhat wider and fur is typically harder to the touch. These characteristics clearly resonate the hard-knock life the American cat endured from the very beginning when it landed on all fours on Plymouth Rock!

Brown tabby American Shorthair owned by Louis and Maricava Johnson.

Red tabby American Shorthair owned by Mary von Paulus.

Probably the most striking physical attribute of the American Shorthair is the animal's symmetry—everything is naturally harmoniously proportioned and placed. This natural quality underscores the whole of the cat. The head is marked by full cheeks and is oblong, though still somewhat longer than wide. A square muzzle and well-formed chin are complemented by a gently sloping nose of medium length. The ears, like those of any regular cat, are medium in size and rounded slightly at the tips, positioned gracefully on the head and wide. The eyes are broad and clear, round with a slight slant—a sure sign of the cat's good health since in this breed the eyes are notably shiny and bright. This is no small cat, tending towards the medium-large, though overall balance and quality are never to be favored over sheer size. The body in its good development is powerful and well knit. The legs are strongly boned with heavy muscle which facilitates the cat's running and jumping and stalking quite nicely. The paws, with heavy pads, ideal for tree climbing, are full and rounded. The tail is not exaggerated and medium-long in length. The Shorthair's coat, of course, is short and has been described as hard in texture; it is sufficiently dense giving the cat surprising protection from the winter cold. The breed standard stresses that the cat should not be overly cobby or rangy and always be of a sensible weight. The activity level of the American Shorthair should ensure that the cat gets sufficient exercise and therefore should never pudge out; likewise, the breed has a healthy appetite and usually avoids looking twiggy.

The American Shorthair tattoos the feline sky with quite an extensive, far-reaching rainbow of colors, including white and black, and even brown. The solid white coat color is glisteningly distinctive, accompanied by deep blue or brilliant gold eyes (or one of each color in the odd-eyed). The solid black cat is as black as coal and night, and its gold eyes sparkle brilliantly in the latter. In the solid blue, a light shade of blue may cover the entire body, and these eyes are gold. An unmarked, unticked red body color richer than bricks with gold eyes is also a solid-color possibility, as is solid cream, buff through and through to its roots.

Black smoke American Shorthair owned by Mary von Paulus.

Color genetics in the American Shorthair are fairly complicated given the complete rainbow of colors the breed can produce. Owner, Solveig M. V. Pfleuger.

Possibly the most recognizable of all cats is the tabby-patterned American Shorthair. Owner, Elaine F. Martin.

Ever popular in the American Shorthair collage are the tabby cats, of which there are three possible patterns, namely the Classic, Mackerel and Patched. Most cat owners view a "Tabby Cat" as a breed unto itself, when in fact it only describes a kind of pattern on a cat. The American Shorthair is hardly unique in possessing these markings, as a great number of other domestic breeds and even some wild jungle cats flash this pelt.

The Classic and Mackerel patterns are markedly similar, with dense and well-defined marks, barred legs, a letter "M" on the forehead, necklaces, and bracelets. Distinguishing the Classic pattern are the vertical dark markings from the back of the head to the shoulders that form a butterfly, the double row of button marks on the chest and stomach, and the evenly ringed tail. The Mackerel pattern exhibits a barred tail, narrow pencil markings around the body and a narrow saddle formed by the spine markings. The Patched pattern can be either of the above but interrupted by patches on both the body and extremities.

The Classic and Mackerel patterns come in a plethora of colors including brown, silver, red, blue, and cameo (which is off-white). The Patched tabby, sometimes called the Tortie

Tabby or playfully the Torbie, comes in silver, brown and blue.

A bicolor body pattern against a white ground color is an attractive and eye-catching possibility. Bicolors can be black, red, blue or cream, all with white.

Beyond the solids, tabbies, and bis, the breed can be found in shaded colors and smokes, which are distinguished by their white undercoats and outer coat markings. Among these possibilities are the shaded silver, chinchilla silver, shell cameo, shaded cameo, cameo or red smoke, black smoke, and blue smoke.

The blue-cream coloration has a blue undercoat marked by clear puddles of cream, while the tortoiseshell pattern with a black undercoat is freckled by patches of both cream and red. There is also a tortoiseshell smoke whose undercoat is white. Similar to the markings of the famed Turkish Van, a van pattern has also been pursued which has auburn markings against a white background.

Lastly, there is a calico cat which has black and red patches against a white ground color. These cats also are mistakenly considered a breed unto themselves, but, like the tabbies, a variety of breeds can be seen in the familiar calico pattern.

The British Shorthair's head should be circular and massive, giving him a rounded forehead with a flattish appearance to the top. Owner, Doane F. Huemmer.

British Shorthair

The isles of Great Britain have always ranked first in producing perfect strains of perfect breeds—the British have always had a knack for creating, establishing, and promoting purebred domestic animals. The British Shorthair, the national cat of England, clearly enjoys this touch of Anglican perfection. Whether or not Roman passers-by, uniformly clad, dropped off baskets of street-tough felines doesn't much substantiate the antiquity of the British Shorthair breed. In truth no breed of domestic cat likely dates back more than a couple hundred years or so. The British Shorthair as a breed was promoted by the father of the cat fancy, as he is commonly regarded, Harrison Weir. Mr. Weir actually followed in the well-placed and thought-out steps of Miss Kit Wilson, who was largely responsible for establishing the purebred strains of the British Shorthair.

Essentially, the common street or garden cats that were seen around England were the cats used to develop the "perfected" British Shorthair breed. On first appearance, any domestic shorthair purebred looks like "any old cat"; largely, what a cat *should* look like, no exaggerated features, harmonious balance, big, clear eyes and an all-weather, shimmering coat of fur.

While the Americans have found it acceptable to not divide the domestic shorthair breed by

Like its cousin, the American Shorthair, the British Shorthair is available in most any pattern and color. This cat is tricolored.

color, the British opt to consider each individual color a separate breed. There is indeed good logic behind this determination, since fanciers through the years have worked diligently in perfecting lines of the individual colors, and color breedings are carefully planned. Despite the British cat council's decision, the British Shorthair is regarded as a single breed in the United States, as is the American Shorthair.

The character of this sturdy British cat we describe as personable yet suitably independent, like many other cats. Appropriately, this cat is not given to extremes. He uses his voice very discreetly, in moderation. The cat is not much prone to coddling yet can be quite given to outbursts of affection. The breed has rightly been called conservative, though more likely the cat will adopt its owner's outlook and lifestyle, provided they are not pushed too far to the right or the left.

In appearance, the British Shorthair breeds enjoy a most sturdy construction. The head, which is circular and massive, is marked by round bone structure with a rounded forehead, giving a flattish plane at the skull top. The nose is broad and medium-sized. The chin is well developed and firm. The stop is notable beyond the whisker pads, which are not overstated. The muzzle is well-developed and strong. The ears are medium in size with round tips set wide apart. The eyes are large and round. This is a medium–large-sized cat with a strong and stocky body, cobby, with excellent musculature. The legs are perfectly sized for the body, powerful with round, firm paws. The tail is medium in length, and tapers to the end;

the tail base is thick. The cat's coat is short and dense, resilient and suitable for outdoor life. The single coat should never be woolly.

The colors of the British Shorthair divide the breeds. The appearance of these different breeds differs only by color of the coat and eyes.

BRITISH BLACK SHORTHAIR

What can be more distinctive, haunting and eye-catching than a sleek solid-black cat with bright copper-colored eyes? The black coat is described as black to the root; the nose and paw pads are also black. Kittens may seem a little rusty, but by six months of age, a show-specimen kitten will be solid black. This is one of the oldest varieties of the British Shorthair and was exhibited early in the days of the Crystal Palace show.

BRITISH WHITE SHORTHAIR

The color should be as white as snow, without any tinge of gray or yellow. The varieties of this breed are odd-eyed, orange-eyed, and blue-eyed. All three varieties have pink paw and nose pads. Commonly white street cats will have green eyes. The odd-eyed White cat resulted from breeders' attempts to perfect the orange-eyed variety. Oddly enough, the cat may be deaf only on the blue-eyed side.

The British Blue Shorthair is a handsome cat with great similarities to the Chartreux, a like-colored cat breed of France. Owner, Kathie Prywitowski.

Blue-eyed Whites frequently suffer from hearing disorders; ideally, the orange-eyed cats do not.

BRITISH CREAM SHORTHAIR

A lush pale cream coloration, not too red, has stumped breeders for years; previous to the mid-twentieth century, Cream was an accident, a serendipitous one, and breeders commonly charged the milkman's cat. The paw and nose pads are pink. Generally, the cream coloration appears like a soft-orange tabby in hiding. The eyes can be Welsh gold, copper or orange; hazel eyes are not desirable.

BRITISH BLUE SHORTHAIR

This blue breed appears a great deal like the Chartreux of France, and sometimes that breed is considered a legitimate member of this British race. Blue, in cat talk, is a medium gray color. The nose pad and paw pads are blue too. The eyes should be copper in color, beautifully contrasting from the solid blue coat color. Blue Persians and Black British Shorthairs are sometimes employed to preserve the genuine blue in some breeding programs. World War II interrupted the breeding programs of the Blue, so not until the mid-1950s did the British Blues land back on their blue paw pads.

BRITISH BLUE-CREAM SHORTHAIR

This cat can be described as a British Blue that the milkman has tossed a saucer of cream (Cream) upon. A pale and subtle

The British Tortoiseshell Shorthair has voluminous, deep copper eyes.

intermingling of these two colors produces the ideal Blue-Cream Shorthair. The eyes are copper, orange, or rich gold. Tortoiseshells are used in breeding programs and litters may contain Creams, Blues and Blue-Creams. The sex-linked gene does not promise longevity for the breed.

BRITISH TABBY SHORTHAIR

A handsome Tabby can't be resisted, in any color. The British club recognizes the tabby in three colors: red, silver and brown; American clubs register blue and cream in addition to these three. Two tabby patterns are known: Mackerel and Classic. The Mackerel pattern is the more striped pattern with the spiraling effect which characterizes the Classic pattern. In each color, pads are similarly colored. The eyes in the Red Tabby are gold or copper in color; in the Silver, they can be gold, orange or hazel; in the Brown, they are dark copper or orange.

BRITISH TORTOISESHELL SHORTHAIR

The tortoiseshell pattern is in fact a tricolor, with well-broken patches of color. There are two additional varieties of this well-liked Briton: the Tortoiseshell and White and the Blue Tortoiseshell and White (this latter is called the Dilute Calico in the States). The Tortie, as he is called, proves difficult to breed, despite the seemingly random, but distinctive, patches of red, black and cream. To acquire a good Tortoiseshell, usually a solid-colored stud (of one of the three patched colors) is mated to the Tortie queen. The Tortoiseshell and White, formerly called the Chintz, is usually acquired by mating a Bicolor to the Tortie and White queen. Paw pads on the Tortie are pink or black (or a combo); the nose pad is black; on the Tortie and White, the nose is black, the paw pads pink; in the Blue Tortie and White, the nose and paw pads are pink or blue.

BRITISH SPOTTED SHORTHAIR

Three possible varieties of the Spotted breed are red, silver and brown in color. Ideally the Spotted Shorthair has an attractive and varied array of rosettes and ovals which embellish the coat tapestry. The Spottie is often categorized as a Mackerel Tabby, except that the markings are exclusively spot-like. The Silver Spottie has green or hazel eyes, with red nose pads, all outlined in black; paw pads are red or black. The Red Spottie has deep orange or red eyes, with pink pads on nose and paws. The Brown Spottie has dark copper eyes.

BRITISH BICOLOR SHORTHAIR

White cats with patches of another color are called Bicolors. Four recognized possibilities or varieties include

British Bicolored Shorthair in Blue and White owned by MJ Eger and MJ Osborne.

the Black and White, called the Magpie; the Blue and White; Red and White; and Cream and White. The white ground should cover ideally no more than one-half of the cat; and the patches never more than two-thirds. While bicolored shorthairs have existed for as long as shorthairs themselves, these cats were principally moggies and only in recent times have "purebred" Bicolors been exhibited at cat shows. Pads on all these cats are pink or the color of the cat's patches.

BRITISH SMOKE SHORTHAIR

Black and Blue Smokes pour forth from this Shorthair's chimney. Like smoke, the color tends to blend in with its background, giving this color a unique effect. A Tortoiseshell Smoke is presently being promoted in Britain, though that smoke hasn't crossed the Atlantic as of yet. The tipping on the cat makes this cat distinctive; double coated, the undercoat is white and the outer coat is tipped in black.

BRITISH TIPPED SHORTHAIR

This unique color was created by combining Smokes, Blues and Silvers, and was originally named the Chinchilla Shorthair. A variety of tips are allowed, including all British colors, plus chocolate and lilac.

British Tipped Shorthair possesses lovely silver tipping over his pure white coat. Owner, Doane F. Huemmer.

British Shorthair in cream-spotted tabby and white owned by the Huemmers.

The long, tapering wedge of the Siamese cat's head appears in perfect proportion to his long, tubular body. The head enjoys complete harmony of all its parts.

Siamese

Long basking in legend and lore, the Siamese hails as *the* cat of the Orient and survives as a prototypical domestic feline. His name derives from his land of origin, namely Siam, today called Thailand, where his inner strength and outward pride enamored the people of this Far Eastern land. Today the Siamese continues to enamor cat fanciers the world over with his harmonious lines, svelte construction, renowned intelligence and far-seeing blue eyes. The Siamese has long been among the most popular of all cat breeds and is called by some "the best known cat in the world." The Siamese makes an ideal choice for many of today's cat lovers, but purchasers should first consider the Siamese character to determine if they are truly fit for ownership.

The intelligent Siamese can dazzle one with its inquisitiveness and problem-solving ability. No challenge is too great, and no death-defying act too dangerous. This is not to say that these cats are problem cats, for truly are they endlessly delightful to the proper owner. These cats need plenty of challenges and regular stimulation. And unlike some other cat breeds, the Siamese

Siamese kitten ready to share his royal heritage with you.

Many Siamese fanciers today believe that the Siamese cat brings peace and security to the home in which he lives. This seal point is owned by Virginia Blackwood.

thrives on human companionship. They are definitely people (often times one-person) cats, a characteristic firmly developed over centuries of cohabitance with man.

A soulful sentinel, the age-old Siamese was believed to protect temples and royal homes from the spirits of evil. He was a most highly prized possession, one forbidden to all but the highest classes of Siam—priests and nobles— and it was believed that he who received (or dubiously acquired) one of these cats would have good fortune bestowed upon him.

The high regard granted the Siamese no doubt has been for the betterment of the breed. These cats were well fed, affectionately handled, and thoughtfully accommodated—conditions which few other breeds of cat have enjoyed with any great consistency through their history. Additionally, and perhaps most importantly, these cats were bred selectively, if only in a relative sense when compared to the genetically founded breeding practices of today; but, nonetheless, they were mated intelligently by people who cared dearly for them. This proper care and breeding have given modern man a cat of great "substance," meaning a cat of desirable and consistent characteristics.

The Western World did not have the honor of the Siamese "experience" until the late nineteenth century. As best as written history can direct us, the breed charted its first transcontinental voyage under the care of Owen Gould, English Counsul-General, who received these first cats as gifts from the King of Siam. While today's Siamese is considerably more refined than the Siamese of 100 years ago, these first cats from Siam differed greatly from the rather cobby domestic shorthairs and Persians of the British Isles, and they were received with the intrigue and fascination that strikes many a Westerner as he considers for the first time the Eastern philosophies of that far-off region of the world.

So impressed has the Western World been with the ever-dazzling Siamese cat that new breeds and colors are constantly hybridized from Siamese stock. These new breeds and colors upset many traditional fanciers, but many cat lovers

The Siamese is prized for his playfulness and animation. This Siamese is owned by Kathleen Comstock.

embrace such developments with open arms.

The refined, tapering lines of the Siamese body; the long, tapering, wedge-shaped contours of the head; the almond-shaped eyes, slanted harmoniously with the lines of and suburban homes of English-speaking peoples. This popularity was not a fad, and we continue today to appreciate keenly this mysterious cat of the Orient, dubbing him the "Sacred Siamese" and preserving his conformation and character.

Siamese kittens get their manners and markings from their mother. Owner, Alice Angermeyer.

the head and ears captured the Western cat fancy. It was not long before representatives of the breed reached America, via a similar route in 1878, also as gifts from the King, and the breed was well received in the U.S.

From the onset, the Siamese grew geometrically in popularity. Soon the breed comprised a major faction at all-breed shows and stood as a watchful guardian over numerous urban

Many a domestic breed would have crumbled under the pressure exerted by popular appeal, especially one so scarce. Unknowledgeable breeders, unknowing owners, and simply base profiteers inevitably take their toll on a burgeoning breed—and the Siamese is no exception. Crossed eyes, nervousness, and simple poor conformation are all documented problems of the breed. However, these cats

The Siamese has a well-muscled body and is finely boned. Like most other cats, the Siamese is extremely agile and light on his feet.

are the exceptions, and the core of the Siamese today remains the hardy, intelligent, and noble cats of yesterday. The potential purchaser of a Siamese must shop carefully: breeding stock should be reviewed and references should be acquired. This word of warning should in no way dissuade the purchaser of a Siamese, for truly these are among the finest of all cats.

The Siamese is a product of over a century of selective breeding which has accentuated the features of the cat that so captivated Western eyes.

However, true today as it was 100 years ago, the Siamese's most distinguishing feature is his graceful and harmonious whole. The Siamese body is long, tubular, and hard. Solid but never bulky, he is a well-muscled cat of fine bone. His head, of course, is shaped as a long, tapering wedge, which is in perfect proportion to the body. The ears of the breed are large, so as to better perceive any spirits that may encroach upon his caretaker's dwelling. The ears are noted for their large base, tapering to a pointed tip.

Regardless of the color of your Siamese, he will have the same fine temperament and affectionate nature. Owner, June Shatto.

The tapering lines of the ears should blend harmoniously with the lines of the wedge-shaped head. The almond-shaped eyes are slanted in classic Oriental fashion, and the lines of their slant should also blend with those of the ears and head. It is unfortunate that uncareful breeding of this high refinement has resulted in such conditions as crossed eyes and "shimmering," a condition in which the eyes seem to vibrate in their sockets. These characteristics are serious faults in the breed, and cats possessing them should never be bred. The tail of the Siamese is long and thin, tapering to a fine point and adding to the overall long appearance of the cat. The legs, also in perfect proportion to the overall whole of the cat, are long, slim, and fine in bone.

The lynx-pointed Siamese cats add many color possibilities to the breed. These Siamese are sometimes registered as Colorpoint Shorthairs. Owner, Suzanne P. Hansen.

In color the Siamese always and forever will occur in the four traditional pointed colors of seal, chocolate, blue, and lilac. By "pointed" it is meant that these colors occur at specific locations (or points) on an otherwise solid-colored or shaded cat. The colorpoints of the Siamese occur on the head, legs and tail. The classic colorpoint of the Siamese is the seal, which is a very dark brown. The first written records of the breed tell of a "fawn-colored creature with jet black legs," which in fact were deep seal brown. The seal point Siamese has a base color of pale fawn to cream, which shades to lighter tones on the underparts of the cat.

The second Siamese color to occur in the West was the blue point, which is believed to have first occurred in England in 1896. Its validity of being truly Siamese was first questioned, but it was then recognized as a natural color mutation. (Today there is still

The chocolate point Siamese is one of the four traditional color points of the breed. Owner, Debbie Legrand.

debate over these original blue cats due to the Korat, another shorthaired Oriental breed from Thailand.) The colorpoints of the blue are not surprisingly described as a deep blue. They occur on a bluish white base color that shades to white on the underparts.

The chocolate point when it first occurred was thought of as a faulty seal point, but like the blue it was soon recognized as an independent color mutation. The chocolate points are described as milk chocolate in color, and they occur on a base color of ivory, which, in contrast to the seal point's fawn/cream,

Seal point adult and kitten owned by June Shatto.

has no shading but is a solid and uniform coloration.

The lilac is a diluted form of chocolate, and it too occurred as an independent mutation. The lilac points are described as frosty gray of pinkish tone, occurring on an unshaded glacial white base color. In all colors, the eyes of Siamese are blue.

In addition to these four traditional colors, many additional colors occur. (Purchaser beware, abundant politics surround these additional colors.) Depending upon the registry, these additional colors are either all considered as Siamese or designate the cat possessing them a Colorpoint Shorthair, a breed separate from the Siamese. Great Britain recognizes most colors, while American registries consider the

additional varieties as Colorpoint Shorthair.

The conflict arose when the aforementioned natural mutations encouraged breeders to seek even more color varieties through limited outcrosses to other breeds, including Abyssinian and domestic shorthairs. This cross-breeding, though somewhat limited, outraged many breeders, who then drew the line that included only the four traditional colors. Today the dissension remains. The additional colors are: red, cream, seal-lynx, chocolate-lynx, lilac-lynx, red-lynx, seal-tortie, chocolate-tortie, blue-cream, lilac-cream, seal-tortie-lynx, chocolate-tortie-lynx, blue-cream-lynx, lilac-cream-lynx, and cream-lynx.

Lynx point Siamese owned by Suzanne P. Hansen.

Arguably one of the world's most ancient cat breeds, the Abyssinian today enjoys a renaissance of interest and enthusiasm in the cat fancy. Owner, Gail Christie.

The Abyssinian's coat shimmers in the light, capturing all the mystique of ancient Egypt. Owner, Lauren Castle.

Abyssinian

With panther-like grace he moves; his large, brilliant eyes focus, his iridescent coat shimmers under the setting Egyptian sun—truly the Abyssinian bears unmistakable mystique. The Aby believably traces to the ancient cats of Egypt, once called Abyssinia. The Egyptians were among the first to domesticate cats, thus making the Aby possibly the oldest of all cat breeds.

The Egyptians revered their domestic felines, seeing in them the symbolic power of the lion. The Egyptian goddess Bastet, who represented the benevolent powers of the sun, was portrayed with a cat's head, and Re, her father and god of the sun, was depicted as a very large cat who slew Apop, the serpent of darkness. To the ancient Egyptians, the cat promised that light would follow dark. And the Egyptians' reverence for the cat brought about the first petite feline companions.

Ancient Egyptian artifacts and hieroglyphics strongly resemble the Abyssinian breed, and the Aby today looks very much like the small native cats of Africa and Asia Minor. The Abyssinian of today is an exceedingly intelligent, very able-bodied cat of gentle temperament and good rapport with humans. He is considered among the most distinct of all breeds, and this distinction has led breeders to use Aby

Although the Aby is no longer regarded as a god, his keepers rightly adore him. Owners, Denise Ogle-Donahue and Kent Fleming.

"blood" to enhance other breeds.

The Aby's basic conformation is foreign, meaning that he is lithe and refined. His head forms a modified wedge, with rounded contours. His ears are large, alert and moderately pointed. And his expressive almond-shaped eyes are brilliant and large. Body is medium-long, firm and muscular yet lithe and graceful. His long tapering tail and proportionately long, slim legs add the finishing features that combine to present a cat of distinction.

Among his most noted features is the uniquely tipped coat, which occurs in four possible colors—ruddy, sorrel, blue, and fawn. The classic ruddy has orange-brown hairs ticked with two or three bands of either black or dark brown, with the extreme outer tip being the darkest. Even the shortest of hairs have at least one band of ticking. The sorrel, also called cinnamon, is a dilution of the ruddy and has warm sorrel-red hairs ticked with chocolate brown. The blue comprises warm soft blue-gray hairs ticked with deeper blue; the base hair and under side are a pale cream color. The fawn involves warm pinkish buff hairs with a powdered effect, ticked with a deeper shade of the same; base hair and under side is a pale "oatmeal." In all colors, the eyes can be gold, copper,

A blue Abyssinian kitten owned by Alyse Brisson.

Abys have great personalities from the start, as this hammy litter reveals. Owner, Alyse Brisson.

green, or hazel, with deep, rich colors desired.

His look of distinction and warm, pleasing character have led to a steady increase in popularity. It was not long ago that the Aby was a very rare breed. Small litters, a preponderance of males, and high price tags on specimens at first hampered the breed's numbers, but today he ranks among the top, with a fervent fancy committed to the breed's betterment. Abys are still not prolific nor easy breeders, and potential owners may well leave propagation to the specialists. But Abys have always been, and still are, hardy and adaptable cats who make a fine choice as pets or

showmen. As with the selection of any popular breed, potential purchasers should shop carefully, ensuring that they get the best cat possible.

Two growing Abys owned by Judith and Cathy Stanton.

Abyssinians grow up to become very noble felines whose resemblance to the great big cats is undeniably alluring. *Kitten* (above) *owned by Sally L. Deegan; adult* (below) *owned by Lauren Castle.*

Abyssinian owned by Denise Ogle-Donahue and Kent Fleming.

The beautiful ivory-ticked Singapura well represents its feline brethren called Orientals. Owner, H. Richbourg.

Given the intelligent and pleasing nature of its Siamese predecessors, the Oriental Shorthair is among the most entertaining of cats. Owners, James J. Bushey and Robert H. Solomon.

Orientals

Graceful and refined, the breeds of the Orient hold a distinctive place in the world of cats, a place perhaps as intriguing as their Far Eastern homeland itself. These breeds are shorthaired cats noted for their tapering lines and harmonious construction. They are perhaps the most intelligent and inquisitive of all cat breeds and serve as excellent choices for potential owners who desire an unabashed, active, and typically vocal breed of cat. Additionally, though they require considerable time spent with their human caretakers—whom these cats often perceive as simple items of amusement—the Orientals described here are all shorthaired breeds with coats that require minimal care and shed considerably less than any of their longhaired counterparts.

The Siamese introduced to the Western World the concept of the Oriental cat in the late 1800s, and ever since his arrival the Far Eastern breeds have been none short on enthusiastic fanciers. Of the Orientals discussed, the Siamese unquestionably contributed blood to the development of at least five. (It is a matter of debate regarding any relationship between the Siamese and his compatriot,

Oriental Shorthair youngsters with wonderfully wild markings. Owner, M. Fabia.

the Korat.) The two breeds clearly independent of the Siamese are the Japanese Bobtail and the Singapura. Taken together, the breeds of the Orient offer cat owners and potential owners awesome possibilities to thoroughly enjoy feline companionship. Taken independently, these breeds provide a good array of colors and variations on a similar conformational theme.

BURMESE

The Burmese has strong ties to the Siamese; it is a hybrid breed that resulted from crosses between an indigenous Asian cat and the Siamese. It was first recognized as a purebred in 1936. Though unquestionably Oriental, the Burmese— especially American-bred cats— presents a more rounded, less svelte and slender appearance than the Siamese. Additionally, the eyes are round and slightly

A playful solid-colored Asian hybrid is the Burmese. Owner, Karen West.

slanted. Yet the Siamese prepotency shines through in the breed, and its general appearance can be considered but a modification of the harmonious Siamese whole. The coat is short, glossy and fine, exhibiting a satin-like texture and look. Originally occurring in sable brown only, the Burmese today also appears in champagne (a warm honey beige), blue, and platinum, with the additional colors of red, cream, and various torties recognized in Great Britain. Definitely Oriental in character, the Burmese demonstrates high intelligence and needs abundant stimulation in the form of play and warm caresses from his human caretakers. His vocal display impresses all cat lovers with its full range of feline purrs and meows. The breed makes an excellent choice for fanciers who perceive the Siamese as being too lithe and refined and would prefer a cat with more "body."

The Burmese comes in a variety of colors beyond the original sable brown. Owner, Maureen Kramanak.

COLORPOINT SHORTHAIR

The Colorpoint Shorthair represents a Siamese in different pointed colors and provides Siamese enthusiasts the perfect opportunity to enjoy the "sacred" experience in a tapestry of "unsacred" colors. The Colorpoint started when the first color mutations of dark brown, chocolate, blue and lilac were witnessed in Western Siamese. Inspired breeders in search of even more colors then crossed in such breeds as the Abyssinian and other shorthairs, which resulted in separate breed status under many registries, especially in the U.S. However, in general appearance and temperament, the Colorpoint Shorthair clearly says "Siamese." The breed possesses a tapering head, notably large ears, and almond-shaped eyes, which are invariably blue. He is constructed of fine bone and firm muscle, and the tail is long, thin and tapering. Colorpoints can be red, cream, seal-lynx, chocolate-lynx, lilac-lynx, red-

This Colorpoint's points are flame. Owners, Charlise Latour and Cher Kelly.

The Oriental Shorthair in a solid color is called a Foreign Shorthair in Great Britain. Owner, Carol Fogarty.

lynx, seal-tortie, chocolate-tortie, blue-cream, lilac-cream, seal-tortie-lynx, chocolate-tortie-lynx, blue-cream-lynx, lilac-cream-lynx, and cream-lynx. The breed is a highly intelligent and very articulate one, qualities consistent with the Orientals and the Siamese in particular. These cats strut proudly and are typically aloof to others of their kind, preferring the autocracy of the homestead.

FOREIGN SHORTHAIR

The Foreign Shorthair is a solid-colored Siamese. It is recognized only in Great Britain, where each solid color variety is granted separate breed status. In the U.S., cats that would be labeled as Foreigns in Britain are considered Oriental Shorthairs, grouped with the smokes, tabbies and other color varieties not recognized as either Siamese or Colorpoint Shorthairs. While technically these cats are hybrids, they are essentially Siamese in type and character, as breeders have competently bred to eliminate all non-Siamese characteristics other than color from the Foreign Shorthair.

JAPANESE BOBTAIL

Named for the land from which the first specimens came to the West, the Japanese Bobtail has long been found throughout various parts of the Far East. His tail mutation provides this cat with a very unique appearance, though his appeal certainly doesn't end here—his inquisitive, docile character and sleek yet substantial construction come packaged nicely in a medium-length coat in an attractive variety of colors. The Bobtail has experienced nearly a century of Western breeding, yet some variation in type still exists. The

Japanese Bobtail bicolor cat in a medium-long coat owned by Marilyn R. Knopp.

typical Bobtail exhibits strong Oriental features, which, however, are not of the Siamese type. He is a more thickly boned

Mi-Ke Japanese Bobtail poses restfully. Owner, Lynn Berge.

cat, though never cobby. The head forms a distinct triangle, with the muzzle considerably broad and rounding to the whisker break. Eyes are rather oval, with a slight Oriental slant. Of course, the bobbed tail is the most distinguishing feature of the breed. It is a natural recessive mutation, which means that tailless-to-tailless matings will produce exclusively tailless offspring. Specific tail type can vary from member to member, with no one type favored over another. No tail, however, should exceed five inches in length. Preferred colors are black, white, and red, either as solid, bicolor, or in the classic and often highly prized tricolor, which is known in Japan as *Mi-Ke*. A tortoiseshell coloration of black, red, and cream also occurs. His approach to life typifies the Oriental cats: lively, witty and curious. The Japanese Bobtail provides endless delights to feline fanciers, and his intelligence is well noted. These cats require plenty of challenging diversions to keep them content and amused.

KORAT

For the owner who seeks the Oriental character and mystique but prefers a cobbier and solid-colored cat, the Korat offers

The Korat is a substantial feline with a mellow, agreeable temperament.

excellent possibilities. Like the Siamese, the Korat hails from Thailand, and it has been argued that the two breeds are more closely related than many conservative fanciers would like to admit. However, while their homelands are the same, their appearances are most different. The Korat is a much more substantial cat. His head is noted for its strong cheek development and broadness between and across the eyes. Ears are large and rounded at their tips. Eye shape is round, suggesting the classic Oriental slant only when partially or fully closed. The well-muscled medium-sized body is best labelled as semi-cobby, which certainly differs from the lithe and refined body of the Siamese. A considerably mellow cat, the Korat is a true contemplator, undoubtedly pondering the mysteries of the East. Adding to its philosophical approach to life, the Korat sports an easycare smooth coat, the color of which is invariably silver-blue. The preferred eye color is dark blue or lavender. The Korat is not your common cat but can be acquired with minimal effort.

A curious group of Oriental Shorthair youths ready for trouble. Owner, Geslot Mepanie.

ORIENTAL SHORTHAIR

Quite simply, in the U.S. the Oriental is a self-colored, shaded, smoke, or tabbie Siamese. In Great Britain, each self color is recognized as a separate breed. The first Oriental Shorthairs occurred in Great Britain when breeders were attempting to produce the Havana Brown. The "accidents" and/or "undesirables" proved quite appealing, and enthusiasts were quick to stabilize the new color varieties. While potential purchasers should consider these cats as identical to the Siamese in type and basic character, it should be noted that the breed is a hybrid, resulting from both spontaneous mutations within the purebred Siamese and color additions introduced from cross-breeding. Selective breeding has theoretically removed all non-Siamese characteristics except the colors to make the breed truly Siamese. As with the Colorpoint Shorthair, the Oriental offers potential owners Siamese delight in an array of different colors and shades.

Tortoiseshell Oriental Shorthair showing great balance. Owner, Cher Kelly.

Two Oriental Shorthairs in very different coat patterns. Owners, James J. Bushey and Robert H. Solomon.

Oriental Shorthair in black and white.

Blue Oriental Shorthair kitten owned by Carol Fogarty.

An intent Oriental in deep contemplation. Owners,
James J. Bushey and Robert H. Solomon.

Red Oriental, alert and playful.

SINGAPURA

A recent Oriental addition to the Western cat fancy, the Singapura has long roamed the streets and rural paths of his native Singapore. Though still few in number, the breed promises to attain at least moderate popularity for its foreign type, uniquely ticked coat pattern, and expressive round eyes. Additionally, the potential for color variation is great, with native Singapore relatives exhibiting every imaginable coat pattern. In the West today, however, only ivory ticked with dark brown is currently recognized. In general appearance, the Singapura is a small- to medium-sized cat, with skull rounded and of good width, tapering in a distinctly foreign manner. Muscle and bone are of sound development, and legs are substantially boned. Tail is slender, not thin, and tapers to a rounded tip. The easycare coat is exceptionally short, fine in texture, and lying close to the body. Shedding is minimal. In character the Singapura is self-maintaining and self-reliant, though his demonstrations of feline affection are clear to those deserving of it. It has been rumored that these cats are aloof and distrusting of humans, but these are mere fabrications or misunderstandings. The Singapura is certainly recommended to cat owners, though acquiring a Singapura will likely prove more difficult than for the better-known Oriental breeds.

The Singapura makes a confident, reliable companion.

The Singapura's eyes are large and almond-shaped, set at a slight angle. Owner, H. Richbourg.

The Tonkinese has rounded eyes and a modified-wedge-shaped head. Owner, Bonnie L. Smith.

The Tonkinese in rich mink. Owner, Geslot Mepanie.

TONKINESE

The Tonk is a breed closely related to the Siamese. He is an American hybrid creation who traces to the 1960s when the Burmese breed was crossed back to the Siamese. It should be noted that the Burmese breed itself is a hybrid that resulted from Siamese crossed with Oriental-type cats. The intention of the founding American breeders was to blend the best Siamese with the best Burmese, to create a cat neither too lithe nor cobby, that is very intelligent and affectionate. His physical characteristics clearly states "foreign." The head, longer than wide, forms a modified wedge, accentuated by a blunt muzzle, medium-sized ears, and rounded eyes. The naturally lustrous coat is silky, short, and close-lying. Color can be any of five shades of mink—natural mink, honey mink, champagne mink, blue mink, or platinum mink—all of which are equally attractive. The Tonkinese makes an excellent choice for a pet and/or an American showman. His beautiful yet undemanding coat adorns any home, and his pleasing character and graceful demeanor bespeak well of his progenitor breeds. Though not the most well known, Tonks are certainly not rare.

Champagne mink Tonkinese.

The hardy yet elegant European
Shorthairs represent the native
shorthaired cats of the Continent.

The Exotic Shorthair in blue: the perfect combination of two of the world's most popular cats, the Persian and American Shorthair. Owners, L. and B. Donaghue.

Other Shorthairs

Easy care and easy temperaments, the shorthairs comprise a distinctive group of cats in the world of domestic felines. The authors have grouped 14 breeds of shorthaired cats in this chapter. They are distinct from the Abyssinian, Siamese, and other Orientals for their more rounded, substantial appearance and non-Eastern heritage. While many have close ties to the prototypical American and British Shorthairs, the Siamese, and the Abyssinian, all are unquestionably their own—the American Wirehair for its distinctive wire coat, the Rexes for their absence of guard hairs, the Ocicat and Egyptian Mau for their spotted coats, the Manx for its lack of tail, and of course the Sphynx for its hairlessness. The list goes on and makes the world of shorthaired cats a truly fascinating one.

Several of these breeds are mutational breeds, the result of independent, spontaneous mutations, which dedicated breeders carefully preserved through selective breeding. Such breeds often display the character of their base breed while offering an appearance quite different from them. A perfect example is the folded-eared Scottish Fold. Others are hybrids, the result of crossing two breeds to achieve a specific appearance, and these breeds often display a blend of character consistent with both parent breeds, for example, the Bombay. A few breeds, such as the Russian Blue and Chartreux, fall into neither category but are purebreds that have believably bred true for centuries. In all, the

The Ocicat is a modern hybrid shorthair whose pelt is reminiscent of the beautiful patterns of the wild cat known as the Ocelot. Owner, Mary Morea.

shorthairs offer a variety of appearances and character, each making the perfect pet for the right owner.

AMERICAN WIREHAIR

Packing the strength of character and body composition of the best domestic shorthairs, the American Wirehair traces to a natural dominant coat mutation that occurred in a litter of shorthaired American farm cats in the mid-1960s. Of the four kittens born in this litter, two displayed this unique wire coat. The dominance of the wire coat over regular short coats helped to develop a substantial breed base. The Wirehair was first recognized by the American registry C.F.A. in 1978, yet remains to be accepted by a British registering body. Over the course of the breed's history, fanciers have developed the Wirehair's conformation along the lines of the American Shorthair while perfecting the unique coat's density and wire quality. Today the American Wirehair stands as a medium- to large-sized, well-rounded cat, appearing cobby and muscular. The head is more rounded than the rather oblong skull of the American Shorthair, but in most other aspects he is similar, occurring in the same myriad of colors as that definitively American breed. Eye color equally varies. His robust, lively disposition is sure to ensure his firm position in the cat world. Potential purchasers should have little difficulty acquiring one of the breed in the U.S. or Canada, but the inexperienced should leave breeding to the professionals.

The American Wirehair's unique coat sets it apart from all other cat breeds: its quality is harsh and wiry. Owner, Herb Zwecker.

BOMBAY

Avid breed fanciers believe the Bombay to be the perfect blend of foreign and domestic feline qualities—provided that jet black is the preferred coat color. Indeed, the Bombay offers owners a nice combination of East and West, particularly in character. A hybrid, the Bombay was created by crossing the American Shorthair with the Burmese, itself a hybrid of Siamese and an Asian cat. The Bombay is most noted for his large round eyes of yellow or copper and uniform black coat. He is harmoniously constructed, of deceiving substance and strength; he is balanced in the middle between domestic and Oriental, being neither cobby nor very lithe. Head is rounded, with face full, broad between the large rounded eyes, referred to as "new copper pennies." Character is pleasing and potentially surprising. Members of the breed may possess strong

With eyes like "new copper pennies," the Bombay is a striking solid-black cat.

"Shorthair" characters, strongly "Oriental" characters, or both. Purchasers are encouraged to view the parents and their other offspring for hints of likely character.

Bombay owned by Karen West.

The Chartreux is a well-mannered feline that only occurs in solid blue. Owner, Fred Andrews.

CHARTREUX

Soft and blue, the Chartreux exhibits a unique conformation and colorful history. He is a distinctly rounded cat, with a broad round head and full cheeks; substantial bone and muscle; and a dense, medium-short, plush coat, which is invariably a shade of blue-gray. Of course, the Chartreux is not the only blue breed, which in part accounts for its debated ancestry. The most commonly accepted theory gives France as the breed's origin, with French cultivation attributed largely to Carthusian monks. Others point to the Russian and British Blues and question the French theory. Regardless of its interesting history, the Chartreux offers modern cat fanciers a cat of even and mellow temperament; pleasingly soft and rounded conformation, accentuated by golden copper eyes, and a blue-gray coat.

CORNISH REX

Among the most distinctive of all cat breeds are the Rexes. The two commonly recognized ones are the Devon and the Cornish Rexes, who have attained their unique appearances through natural genetic mutations of their coat. The Cornish was the first of the two breeds, occurring in a litter of domestic English cats in 1950. Breeders then crossed the affected offspring back to the mother, thus better establishing the mutation. From this first breeding come all Cornish Rexes. This Cornish coat mutation has resulted in an absence of guard hairs and reduced awn and down hairs that have become curly and wavy. Additionally, while they are of domestic origin, the Rex breeds exhibit a foreign, or Oriental, appearance. The Cornish body is slender and has a rather arched look; head is relatively small and narrow,

Despite the Cornish Rex's peculiar coat type, he is your average playful cat through and through. Owner, Theresa Rappa.

forming a medium wedge; ears, large; eyes oval, with slight upward, Oriental slant. There is no shortage of possible colors, as solids, shadeds, smokes, tabbies, and other color variations occur. The Cornish Rex is well known as an active, entertaining cat, with a lively springy air and renowned jumping ability. His distinctive coat has no unordinary grooming demands, though breeding should be left to the specialists.

The large pixie-like ears of the Cornish Rex give him a distinct look. Owner, Theresa Rappa.

The Cornish Rex's coat is curly and wavy and can be seen in a many amazing, technicolor hues. Owner, Babette Gray.

That the Devon Rex has guard hairs makes it significantly different than its Cornish cousin. Owners, Don and Diane Moran.

DEVON REX

Like his Cornish cousin, the British-born Devon Rex resulted in a natural genetic mutation of the coat. The Devon mutation occurred in the 1960s. It was a different mutation, and the Devon is a completely separate cat from the Cornish, to which it should never be bred. Unlike the Cornish coat, the Devon's does have guard hairs, though they are reduced and appear to be absent. Overall, the coat is wavy (as in the Cornish), very sparse and somewhat coarse. The general appearance of the Devon is Oriental, with a slender and racy construction, wedge-shaped skull, large ears, and slightly slanted eyes. Overall, he is more lithe than his Cornish cousin. Coat color is varied, offering fanciers an abundance of choices. Grooming needs are basically similar to those for any other shorthaired cat, with the exception that a more delicate hand should do the stroking as the guard hairs are rather brittle. As with other mutational felines, breeding should be left to the experts.

Devon Rex epitomizing alertness and inquisitiveness. Owner, Ralph A. Covert.

EGYPTIAN MAU

The Egyptian Mau offers a truly exotic appearance and a truly exotic name. His most distinguishing feature is his immediately impressive, attractively spotted coat, which adorns an overall body type similar to the native domestic cats of Egypt. But while his name and conformation point to the Pyramids, his actual development occurred in America during the 1950s and '60s from carefully breeding cats imported from Cairo. His head is slightly wedge-shaped, with conspicuously large ears, and large, nearly round eyes. The body, lithe and refined, suggests a well-muscled Oriental type. Legs are long and lean. Tail is medium in length. The Mau is slow to mature as a kitten. But once his adult coat and character emerge, little is left for the owner to desire in a companion cat or a stunning showman. The voice of this cat is described as a pleasant chirping, and overall he is an intelligent and affectionate feline.

A cat undeniably his own: an Egyptian Mau can never change his spots! Owner, Kaye Chambers.

EXOTIC SHORTHAIR

The ultimate representative of Persian–American Shorthair crosses, the Exotic Shorthair exhibits Persian conformation in an attractive, shorter coat, and perhaps the perfect blend of character that fanciers assert is the best of both these ever-appealing breeds. The breed started in the mid-1900s when American Shorthair breeders began crossing to the popular Persian to adjust the type of the domestic breed. This outcrossing was met with strong disapproval by breed conservatives, but the resultant cats were so attractive that breeders maintained and refined this new hybrid cat, which achieved breed status in the late 1960s. Today the Exotic Shorthair should display all the physical qualities of the Persian, except for coat. He is cobby in type, with a well-rounded head and very broad skull; his face is characteristically Persian, with his short, broad nose and large, full eyes, set far apart. The coat is like the American Shorthair's, though longer. Possible colors can be just about any cat color, including those recognized by the Shorthair and the Persian, with few exceptions. Outcrossing to the Shorthair and Persian still occur, and character can sway more towards either breed, or be uniquely Exotic—docile yet independent, determined yet cooperative, affectionate yet aloof. In all, the Exotic Shorthair offers the perfect blend of cat for many feline fanciers. A longhaired variety, known as the Exotic Longhair is recognized in Canada.

Exotic Shorthair adult and kitten in bicolored patterns. Owner, Le Diagorn.

Above: *The Exotic Shorthair is a sturdy, cobby cat with much personality. Owner, Joann Miksa.*
Right: *Exotic Shorthair sitting pretty. Owner, Linda Darville.*
Below: *Exotic Shorthair in a dramatic black and white pattern. Owner, Susan Marshall.*

HAVANA BROWN

Havanas are essentially hybrid Siamese. Domestic Shorthair and Russian Blue blood can also be found in the breed. The Havana was specifically created in Britain during the mid-1900s for its solid brown, glossy coat and Oriental appearance. It is a well-known cat in both America and Great Britain, though type differs in the two countries. If you desire a strongly Siamese type, select a British-bred Havana, as American breeding has selected for a less svelte appearance. In either case, the Havana suggests the foreign, with a wedge-shaped head; wide, tapering ears; and almond-shaped eyes that are slanted in typical Oriental fashion. Legs are long and gently thin, and tail is long and tapering. The coat of the Havana is short, very glossy, exhibiting a satin-like quality, and the hallmark coat color is brown of a rich chestnut shade. The breed's lively and outgoing personality reveals the Siamese, while its fearless curiosity suggests the domestic. In all, the Havana is probably the perfect cat for those who appreciate rich chocolate and entertaining companions.

The Havana Brown is named for its rich chestnut brown coat, the color of a good Cuban cigar. Owners, Richard and Lori Bilello.

MANX

Unique in the world of cats for his lack of tail, the Manx traces to an ages-old unrecorded mutation—occurring possibly in the Far East, possibly off the coast of England, possibly elsewhere. This mutation has affected not only the cat's tail but also his general rear-end construction, which rises higher than the rest of his body, with hind legs much longer than the fore. Additionally, the mutation has been linked to some genetic abnormalities, prenatal deaths and other problems. However, a Manx of good breeding is a really fine cat. In general appearance, the Manx sports a compact, sturdy, well-balanced construction. The degree of taillessness can vary and is broken down into four categories: 1. Rumpy-riser, having a few vertebrae; 2. Stumpy, having longer, often kinked or deformed tail; 3. Longie, having a tail shorter than full length but longer than other Manx types; and 4. True Manx, having an absolute lack of tail. Of course, the true Manx is the ideal Manx. He is a double-coated cat, with short undercoat and slightly longer outer coat, which can occur in any color except the Siamese (Himalayan) points. A long-coated variety known as the Cymric also exists. The Manx personality is hard to label in concrete terms because cross-breeding to normal-tailed breeds is necessary to prevent abnormalities. In general, they are pleasing, typically feline felines. Manx are slow to mature.

This tailless wonder of the cat world derives from the Isle of Man: the Manx. Owner, Victoria Marks.

A relatively new breed, the Ocicat mesmerizes cat people with his wildly spotted coat. Owner, Patti Fraumeni.

OCICAT

The Ocicat is among the lesser known of the shorthaired breeds. A recent hybrid, the Ocicat resulted from Abyssinian–Siamese–American Shorthair crosses, and the name "Ocicat" was selected because the breed's attractive spotted coat coloration resembles that of the ocelot, a South American wild cat. In general appearance, the Ocicat, though a large cat, tends towards the foreign, and continued Aby crosses (the only crosses allowed) will likely increase this tendency. The Ocicat today has a modified wedge-like skull; large ears; slightly slanted eyes; and rather slender, long-bodied construction. The most important feature of the coat's coloration is the distinctively spotted agouti pattern, which may occur in any of twelve colors, including six shades of silver, tawny, brown tabby, chocolate, cinnamon, soft brown, blue, lavender, and fawn. The Oci offers potential owners a truly impressive cat of good size, foreign construction, and spotted coloration. His temperament dictates plenty of space, coupled with goodly amounts of both human companionship and independent problem-solving.

Good looks and charming ways too. Owner, Patricia Clarke.

137

The Russian Blue is one of the most demonstrative of cats, not to mention handsome and creative. Owners, David and Karen Boyce.

RUSSIAN BLUE

The Russian Blue is not just a short-coated blue cat with a name pointing it to the East. It is truly a distinctive cat that, as best as history comes to us, descends from Russian shorthairs of centuries ago. Unlike the domestic shorthairs of England and America, the Russian Blue should never appear cobby. Though well-muscled and solid, the Blue's body is graceful, of fine bone, and good length. Head is wedge-shaped, more so in Great Britain. Ears are large, with rounded tips, set less vertically on the head in the U.S. Eyes are rounded, with a deep green color characteristic of the breed. Of course, the Blue's hallmark is his clear, even, bright blue coat, with lighter shades typically preferred in the U.S. The character of the Russian Blue is best described as peaceful and easy. He enjoys the company of people and is inclined to show great affection towards his owner. The Blue also enjoys moments on his own, when he can contemplate his own unwritten history, lost forever to time.

SCOTTISH FOLD

With the only folded ears in catdom, the Scottish Fold has undoubtedly found an inextricable place in the feline fancy. His unique folded ears are the product of a spontaneous mutation that occurred in a litter of Scotch farm cats in the 1960s. This ear mutation is dominant over normal ears, and propagation must proceed through crossing to erect-eared cats, as fold-to-fold crosses have shown a direct correlation to some physical malformations. In general appearance he is a medium-sized, well-rounded cat—never cobby or coarse—with a broad, round head; round, well-padded body; and legs which give the appearance of shortness. Tail length can vary from medium to long, with longer and more tapering preferred. Demonstrating a myriad of possible colorations, the short, densely coated Fold can occur in all the same colors as the American Shorthair. And his character, too, can be likened to the domestic shorthairs from which he originated—hardy, demonstrative, active, and intelligent. Some Folds may demonstrate rather strong independence, but all are warmly affectionate. Of course, breeding by other than specialists is strongly discouraged. A Longhair variety has also taken hold in the States.

The Scottish Fold is a mutant whose funny folded ears give him an irresistible appeal.

The Scottish Fold comes in all of the colors we find in American Shorthairs. These are hardy, happy cats that love the attention of their people. Owners, Gwen Hornung and Noni G. Ehrola.

The Sphynx cat is by far the most unique cat in the world: the only hairless cat breed. A great hypoallergenic choice for cat lovers. Owner, Sandra Adler.

SPHYNX

Though commonly grouped with the shorthairs, the Sphynx commands a class all his own. He is a hairless cat, the only hairless feline in the world, and for this fact he is most unique. The breed, and breeders of it, have stirred great controversy in the cat world. Because the hairless mutation is a recessive one, some fanciers fear that the trait could be unknowingly introduced and carried undetected in non-hairless lines. However, the Sphynx's human family feels very strongly about the breed and adamantly breeds to high standards. For the owner in search of a true eye-raiser and the ultimate conversation piece in an intelligent and affectionate feline, the Sphynx may be the ideal choice. Additionally, the breed may offer allergy-suffering cat fanciers that long-yearned-for opportunity to own a feline, though typically the retail price of these cats is not cheap. In general appearance, the Sphynx exhibits foreign qualities, both because the mutation has affected type and due to early Siamese crosses to the breed. Head appears rather small; ears, large and triangular; eyes oval and inclined outwards. Body is slender, with medium-length legs and long, hardly tapering tail.

The hairless Sphynx began as an accident, a mutation, but today he has many intentional admirers. Owner, Sandra Adler.

Experiments, Accidents, and Immigrants

Any community has a trickling of mutants and imported oddities—and the cat world is no exception. While the feline physique is exceptional in its consistency and dexterity, slight "imperfections"on that delightful canvas never fail to turn a head. Turning one's head, while not truly polite or politically correct, is acceptable—staring, guffawing, and drooling at a slight imperfection are not. Unfortunately, too many cat folk stare, guffaw, and drool at any passing X-kittens (aka teenage mutant cats). Any mutation, no matter how slight or extreme, merits celebrating, breeding, registering, and eventually trademarking. The lack of a tail, half a tail, frizzy fur, curled ears, short forepaws, a quirky color, no hair, wire hair, bent hair, etc., etc., indicate genetic mutations—not miracles or divine intervention.

Cat folk, especially insatiable Americans, greet the unusual with open arms and pocketbooks—provided that it's not human. From these variants of nature or human-imposed oddities, a growing, rather intriguing fraternity of felines has evolved, or been forced to evolve. While mutations have been around as long as life itself

The Ragdoll is the colorful creation of Ann Baker, one of the world's most renowned cat breeders and inventors. Owners, Kim Brantley and Bob Balas.

on this planet, among the first feline mutants we know is the Sphynx, the world's first hairless cat breed. This hairless flowerchild occurred in Canada during the mid-60s. The persistence and faith of early Sphynx breeders should convert all unbelieving cat fanciers (and sardonic authors) of this naked child's worth. Today's breed is quite a handsome, well-balanced cat, a millennia ahead of the earliest breed specimens whose frames and faces were contorted and terribly unlike. Despite its convincing nudity, the confident Sphynx has not quite found Eden in the '90s, as only the Canadian club recognizes the breed and few

cats can be seen in the States. Pet Sphynx, of all cats, would be kept indoors, so we never see one of these hanging out in the alleyway. Controversy also persists in cat circles since the hairless trait is linked to a recessive gene and can be carried undetected by seemingly normal-furred cats.

A new wave in the cat world broke on shore in the 1950s with the Cornish Rex—and again a decade later with the Devon Rex. An absence of guard hairs, with few awn and down hairs, produced a wavy, near curly coat, which caught the eye of British fanciers in Cornwall and Devon. The rex mutation was known in rabbits

The Selkirk Rex is a recent mutation, possessing the curly coat of the Rex breeds on the cobby body of a Persian. Owner, Solveig M. V. Pfleuger.

A dramatic Selkirk Rex in solid black. Note the very prominent curly whiskers. Owner, Jeri L. Newman.

previously and, since these feline rex mutations occurred on different gene loci, different results occurred, and different breed status was maintained. Little known cat wonders such as the German and Oregon Rex varieties have also been heralded; these crinkly coated kitties are similar to the Cornish Rex.

Following the rex routine is yet another newcomer to the cat world, the Selkirk Rex. This breed, as it were, possesses a typical cobby shorthair body with a rex-wavy coat. Both the Devon and Cornish breeds have longer, foreign-type bodies. Likely the Selkirk resulted from crossing a Devon with an American Shorthair. The result is a fairly handsome, and seemingly hardy new cat.

The American Shorthair has also yielded another mutant in the American Wirehair, a cat with a rough, wiry coat.

The Nebelung is the longhaired variety of the Russian Blue. Owner, Cora Cobb.

Coat variants and mutations have become very common in the cat world. It has become unusual for any well-loved shorthaired breed not to have a longhaired adopted brother, or at least a cousin once-removed. The Siamese has two such relations: the Balinese and Javanese; the Abyssinian has the much-loved Somali; the Scottish Fold and Oriental Shorthair, variants in their own rights, have the Longhaired Scottish Fold and Oriental Longhair; the Manx—"never mind anyway that's another story"—has the Cymric and most recently, the Russian Blue has his longhaired Wagnerian counterpart in the Nebelung.

Cat folk have proven to harbor extreme fetishes with tails, or the lack, or near-lack, thereof. Ever since Noah or Samson violently de-tailed the Manx, tail mutations have abounded. The Japanese Bobtail and Cymric can be counted among the known tailless mutations and most recently the American Bobtail, which derived from a Siamese cross. This little cat has Siamese points and a sweet temperament, even though it is but narrowly promoted in the U.S. Tail mutations are serious since the tail and vertebrae are

The American Bobtail joins the ranks of the other tailless kitties as the newest bobtail on the block. Owner, Alain Guillerme.

inseparable. Breeders have experienced nightmarish crippling in cats in the process of developing this unusual cat. Bobtail mutations, though, are fairly common, yet in many places they are ignored or culled. We understand that there exists a league of tailless Abys in Thailand as well as similar cats in Spain.

Ears also turn heads. Today the cat fancy has tripped head over heels for a couple distinctive felines with ear peculiarities: the Scottish Fold and the American Curl. These cats possess bent, curled or folded ears. The American Curl's ear is actually roundish, giving the cat a peculiar though thoroughly lovable appearance.

Mutations that serendipitously spring up account for only half of the breed developments in today's cat world. Those seemingly innocent natural flukes merely entice their witnesses and maybe inspire them or pique their cat-like curiosity. Other folk intentionally venture forth to create new oddities—to impress their friends, to pay off the mortgage, to flash their

An American Bobtail kitten displaying his bob. Owner, Alain Guillerme.

The Highland Fold, or Longhair Scottish Fold, represents a longhair occurrence in that popular Scottish breed. Owner, Kathleen Comstock.

The Snowshoe derives from a Siamese–American Shorthair cross. The breed is prized for its white snowbooties and beautiful teal-colored eyes. Owner, Doris-Chinn Reese.

name around fancy publications, to become immortal. Of course some of these "discoveries" or inventions are truly worthy and valuable to the endurance of the fancy and show world. The others, as suggested, the cat fancy could wholly survive without.

Creating a new longhair breed or variant seems always to rely on the Persian. A new breed called the Burmilla was created by pairing a chinchilla Persian with a Burmese. This new British breed resulted in a stunning semi-foreign-type body, much like the Burmese. It occurs in many colors, and breeders

from Great Britain have already began exporting to the United States where an open-armed fancy is excited about the new breed.

Another longhaired fur fellow came along in the 1980s. This breed, called the Tiffanie, was also developed from the Burmese and Persian, and essentially looks like a longhaired Burmese. The fur is semi-long, silky and fine; the tail is bushy and the ears are equipped with streamers, as they are called. The coat or body type does not resemble the Persian, nor is the body svelte like a Siamese. Breeders, centered mainly in the States, are concentrating on the Burmese traits so that the breed doesn't resemble a solid-colored Persian (or Kashmir). Breed registries are categorizing the breed as an Asian. Color possibilities include solids in blue, chocolate, black, lilac, red, and cream; tortie varieties are also available.

A more established experimental is known as the Snowshoe, another handsome medium-coated cat, distinguished by its four white paws. This hybrid breed was developed from the Siamese and a bi-colored American Shorthair. The breed's eyes are roundish in shape and tealish in color. The coat is Himalayan in pattern, in seal or blue points. Breeders recognize the difficulty in maintaining this cat's white-as-snow shoes.

The Bengal is a recent attempt to cross a wild cat with a domestic feline. Early attempts at this, such as the Safari, proved to lack much gusto. This breed's creator, Jean Sugden, began the program in 1963, and thus far it has been met with roaring success. The Asian leopard cat was the wild feline in question and the Bengal handsomely displays this wild cat's pelt: in color the breed

Bengals were developed from crosses of domestic cats with small Asian cats. Today the Asian cat is still used to preserve the wild type of the Bengal breed. This is a three-month-old second-generation Bengal bred by Barbara J. Andrews.

can be three shades, leopard (a brown tabby), snow leopard, and marble leopard. This new purebred is surely one of the most attractive cats in town. Unexaggerated and hardy, the Bengal has a medium-short coat which is thick and full. The body is quite large and the tail is thick. The head is a broad modified wedge with rounded contours. Egyptian Maus were originally used for outcrosses, and although today's breed base is stable, small Asian wild cats are still used to keep the wild in the Bengal. First and second generation Bengals may defecate in drinking water as do their wild forebears—owners must raise their bowls to thwart this behavior.

An even newer brand of handsome cat that we've spied upon is the California Spangled, which, like the Bengal, was engineered to resemble a wild spotted cat. This American West-coast sensation is truly a gorgeous animal, and if you can afford to acquire one, by all means do.

The California Spangled is a lovely wild spotted cat who has won many west-coast hearts. Owner, Paul Casey.

The Siberian is an immigrant from Russia, a "husky" outdoor cat with a truly impressive coat.

Another new face in the cat world is nо creation at all, but an immigrant: the Siberian Cat. This "new" breed is indeed an ancient pedigreed cat of Russia. The first three American imports to a Himalayan cat breeder in Baton Rouge, Louisiana, arrived on July 28, 1990, in appreciation for her kind exportation to St. Petersburg to improve Himmy lines in Russia. The breeder's name is Elizabeth Terrell, the first fancier to promote the breed abroad. These cats are not merely any stray Russian cat snagged off the street in St. Petersburg (or purchased for one dollar!), but a distinctive cat with a certified pedigree. In appearance, this Russian looks much like the Norwegian Forest Cat or Maine Coon.

Special things keep happening to Ragdoll creator, Ann Baker—things she calls "miracles". When the Ragdoll popped out of the oven some decades ago, the cat world treaded lightly—unsure of this trademarked newcomer. The Ragdoll, indeed, is a lovely breed that occurs in over a baker's dozen colors. Regardless of findings and published tracts, the breed is not more tolerant of pain than other breeds and the propensity to go limp in one's arms might be considered a defect that would seem undesirable in a responsive pet. (This trait is often bred-for in laboratory rats where it's useful to scientists.)

New specialties out of the Ann-Bakery include the Honeybear and Miracle. Little actual information has been acquired on these breeds. The Honeybear, named for its sweet temperament, is purportedly a genetically engineered cross between a domestic cat and a skunk. The cat, as a result, possesses a tremendous striped skunk-like tail, but of course is not able to spray—thankfully, imagine a cat having a bad day with that mechanism. (Remember when certain unlucky-footed folk were once promoting cabbits, cat–rabbit crosses—these too failed to bounce to the forefront of the pet market.) The Miracle was apparently sent to Baker, much the same way the Angel Gabriel arrived at the Virgin Mary's stoop, though the long-term results of this annunciation seem less likely to interrupt the Earth's revolution.

Breeding is not as mysterious as all this!—and breeds need not be copyrighted for the good of the animals involved.

The Chocolate York with a milk-colored bib.

Experiments, Accidents, and Immigrants

The Munchkin or Creole Kangaroo is to the cat what the Basset Hound is to the dog. These short-forelegged creatures are the first such felines to be bred. Owner, Laurie Bobskill.

Feline experiments in the '90s include three other new breeds: Ojos Azules, a shorthair in various colors and patterns all with *blue eyes*; the Creole Kangaroo (or Munchkin), an odd little Southern mutant with basset-like front legs (no pouch); and the Chocolate York, a thickly furred sturdy longhair in a soft-chocolate and white pattern.

Assuredly, the list of new feline developments, mutations and international finds expands as we speak, as does this universe of cats . . . . .

Ojos Azules, in Spanish "blue eyes," are being bred for their deep blue eyes. The breed comes in many colors. Owner, Laurie Bobskill.

Above: *The latest "ragtype" cat is the Ragamuffin , a strikingly colored and sweet spinoff of the Ragdoll. Owner, Patricia Flynn.* Below: *The LaPerm boasts a unique "curly" coat. The breed was developed from a gray tabby barn cat's litter. The mutant kitten had a curly coat and very big ears. Owners, Laurie Bobskill, Solveig Pfueger and Linda Koehl.*

Munchkin showing off his unique front assembly. Owner, Solveig M.V. Pfleuger.

Index

Index

GREAT CAT BOOKS
FROM TFH

PS-783	PS-736	H-1057	KW-062	KW-061	H-918
160 Pages	160 Pages	128 Pages	96 Pages	128 Pages	271 Pages
50 Color Photos	23 Full Color &	30 Full Color	60 Full Color	Over 100	22 Full Color &
	8 B/W Photos	& B/W Photos	Photos	Color Photos	147 B/W Photos

TS-173	TS-127	TS-136	TS-152
304 Pages	384 Pages	160 Pages	480 Pages
Over 400	Over 300	Over 50	500 Full Color
Full Color Photos	Full Color Photos	Full Color Photos	Photos

The authors' *Mini-Atlas of Cats* is a recommended excellent resource for further reading about the many breeds. More extensive and colorful are *The Allure of Cats* and *The Atlas of Cats of the World.* Your pet shop or book store will have these great TFH cat books as well as other cat breed books for you to see and purchase for your home library.